Young People at Risk

Conservation of Human Resources
Studies in Health Policy

Strategic Factors in U.S. Health Care: Human Resources, Capital, and Technology, Howard S. Berliner

Medicine and Society: Clinical Decisions and Societal Values, edited by Eli Ginzberg

From Physician Shortage to Patient Shortage: The Uncertain Future of Medical Practice, edited by Eli Ginzberg

Young People at Risk

Is <u>Prevention</u> Possible?

Eli Ginzberg,
Howard S. Berliner,
and Miriam Ostow

WESTVIEW PRESS
BOULDER AND LONDON

Conservation of Human Resources Studies in Health Policy

Copyright © 1988 by Conservation of Human Resources, Columbia University

Published in 1988 in the United States of America by Westview Press, Inc.; Frederick A. Praeger, Publisher; 5500 Central Avenue, Boulder, Colorado 80301

Library of Congress Cataloging-in-Publication Data
Ginzberg, Eli, 1911–   .
   Young people at risk.
   (Conservation of human resources studies in
health policy)
   Includes bibliographies and index.
   1. Juvenile delinquency—United States.
2. Juvenile delinquency—United States—Prevention.
3. Drug abuse—United States—Prevention.
4. Pregnancy, Adolescent—United States—Prevention.
5. Dropouts—United States. I. Berliner, Howard S.,
1949–   . II. Ostow, Miriam. III. Title.
IV. Series.
HV9104.G547   1988   364.3'6'0973   87-21557
ISBN 0-8133-0525-X

Composition for this book originated with conversion of the author's computer tapes or word-processor disks.

Printed and bound in the United States of America

The paper used in this publication meets the requirements of the American National Standard for Permanence of Paper for Printed Library Materials Z39.48-1984.

6   5   4   3   2

Contents

Tables and Figures

Preface

This book is a collaborative undertaking among the three authors. Howard S. Berliner had primary responsibility for Chapters 3 and 5 and Miriam Ostow for Chapter 4. I was responsible for Chapters 1, 2, 6, and 7.

We are indebted to the Commonwealth Fund for the grant that underwrote this effort and to Thomas Moloney, the senior vice president, for encouraging us to direct our attention to the challenging question of whether the "prevention paradigm" can be transferred from the health arena to problems of social pathology.

In preparing this book for press we were assisted by Ruth Ginzberg, who gave editorial support; by Penny Peace, who served as the linkage between the Conservation Project and our publisher; and to Sylvia Leef and Shoshana Vasheetz, who transcribed and prepared the multiple versions of the manuscript.

Eli Ginzberg,
Director,
Conservation of Human Resources

1

The Setting

This introductory chapter has a limited number of goals including providing the reader with the background of this undertaking, its place in the ongoing research in human resources and health policy that are the center of the Conservation of Human Resources research program at Columbia University, and the relationships between its findings and public policy aimed at assisting young people at risk.

The origin and purpose of this research effort can be briefly outlined. The Commonwealth Fund, under the leadership of its senior vice president, Thomas Moloney, explored our potential interest in assessing the current efforts of various foundations to reduce ineffective behavior among adolescents such as drunk driving, teenage pregnancy, and dropping out of school. The Foundation specifically considered whether prevention programs held promise of reducing the individual and social costs of disability and death resulting from such destructive behavior.

Many philanthropic sponsors have come to recognize that the conventional medical model of intervention—assisting young people after they have gotten into serious trouble—is both costly and often ineffective. Once the individual has acquired certain values and patterns of behavior, it is difficult or even impossible to change the life-style and injurious consequences associated with that behavior. Hence many conventional therapeutic and rehabilitative interventions appear to yield few positive outcomes.

The growing realization of the limitations of conventional interventions led the Commonwealth Fund and other philanthropic organizations to look hard at the potential of prevention. The tasks given to us were (1) to review the theory of prevention of socially ineffective behavior among adolescents and (2) to assess the record of prevention in a number of problem areas, specifically drunk driving, teenage pregnancy, adolescent drug use, and school dropouts.

Although the Conservation of Human Resources had never focused research specifically on prevention and had only occasionally singled

1

out adolescents as a target group, we believed that the Commonwealth Fund's concern was important and fell within the broad scope of our research interests and capabilities. Accordingly we welcomed the opportunity to explore the problem of the potential of prevention among adolescents at risk.

We note in the following paragraphs some of the Conservation Project's earlier research investigations that bear on the current effort. In our earliest studies of the long-term unemployed, the impact of the father's unemployment on young children and adolescents was singled out for special attention.[1] In our investigations into occupational choice, the focus of our inquiry was the maturation of the choice process during adolescence and young adulthood.[2]

The multiple volumes that emerged from our long-term studies of the military personnel experience of World War II, prompted by General Dwight D. Eisenhower's deep concern with getting the lessons of that experience before the American people, were heavily involved in placing adolescent behavior in the context of long-term developmental sequencing under differing environmental conditions, civilian and military, with primary focus on the assessment of performance in each setting.[3]

In *The Negro Potential*, we addressed for the first time a seriously disadvantaged group and highlighted how inadequate opportunities at home and in school were important precursors of later ineffective performance.[4]

As the chair, Committee of Studies for the Golden Anniversary White House Conference on Children and Youth, I edited a number of volumes that explored various aspects of adolescent experience.[5] The three-volume work, *The Nation's Children*, is being reprinted in 1987 (Transaction Books, Rutgers University, New Brunswick, N.J.) with a new introduction in which I have written a retrospective assessing the extent to which we have responded by the mid-1980s to the agenda of the late 1950s as well as noting the new items that must be added to that agenda.

In 1967 in *The Middle-Class Negro in the White Man's World* my colleagues and I explored the extent to which improved occupational and income status of the families of black men helped to moderate the crippling effects of race on educational and career choices.[6]

In 1980, we published two studies on educational deficiencies and lack of success in the world of work that focused heavily on the problems of minority youth.[7]

For the convenience of the reader I have also noted additional references to monographs and reports of the Conservation Project that relate to the critical issue of the developmental experiences of adolescents and their performance potential.[8]

The foregoing brief references should help clarify that although the developmental problems of adolescents only occasionally were the principal focus of our earlier research, we dealt with aspects of the subject in no fewer than twenty-five of our earlier investigations.

Because the term "ineffective performance" has been used without amplification, we will make explicit the criteria that the Conservation staff developed early in its research program to define effective performance. In an imperfect world in which many individuals and groups have to cope with modest endowments and opportunities we define "effective performance" as follows: the ability of the individual to support himself and his dependents (the definition predates the large increase of women in the labor force and the large rise in the number of female-headed households); to stay out of trouble with the criminal justice system; to enter into and maintain a long-term marital relationship; and to be able if physically fit to serve in the armed forces in a national emergency or war. Although these criteria are assuredly modest, we shall soon see that large numbers of young people are unable to meet them in whole or in part.

The second aim of this introductory chapter is to point up the relationship between the theme of prevention and the four areas of adolescent malfunctioning—drunk driving, teenage pregnancy, drug use, and dropping out of school. The neoconservatives claim that most intervention efforts subsumed under the rubric of the Great Society programs (1964–1968) have failed; witness the large numbers of young people in serious trouble. The counterargument emphasizes that considering the many children who grow up in a one-parent household with income at or below the poverty level, in inadequate housing and deteriorating neighborhoods whose schooling is dysfunctional, the appropriate observation is not the large number of young people who get into serious trouble, but rather the many who are able to escape from their depressive environment. In the last chapter we weigh these opposing views and confront head-on the issue of policy interventions.

Once one looks beyond the macro-forces that impinge heavily on racial minorities and children growing up in single-parent households in or close to poverty, one must note that race and income are not determining factors in accounting for drunk driving among adolescents and young adults. But race, poverty, and single-parent households go far to account for the vast majority of adolescents who become pregnant, use drugs, or drop out of school.

The differences between young people growing up in advantaged versus disadvantaged families are substantial. Adolescents in middle-class families have more options in seeking adventure, acting out and gaining immediate satisfactions, some of which are less injurious than others. The basic advantage family support and more disposable income provide is an extra margin for the young person who gets into trouble. This margin affords him or her a second, or even a third, and a fourth chance to recoup. The seriously disadvantaged seldom have even a second chance.

Finally, from a policy perspective it is becoming increasingly clear to all interested parties—parents, politicians, philanthropists—that if effective human growth and development depend on individual endowment, family support, and societal institutions (particularly educational and employment opportunities), then it is of the utmost importance to ensure that individuals do not fall off the track, or if they do, that they can get back on as quickly as possible. Ours is fast becoming a society in which the absence of functional literacy at a minimum of tenth grade level will preclude most people from an effective role in the world of work. Hence the critical importance of seeing that the frighteningly high dropout rate, particularly among minority youth (between one-third and one-half), is radically reduced by providing many of them special assistance starting as early as their preschool years to ensure that they do not fall behind and eventually fall off the track.

Admittedly, adequate educational preparation is no guarantee that an individual will not engage in ineffective behavior involving sex, drugs, or alcohol. But the obverse formulation has even greater pertinency: The young adult with inadequate educational preparation will experience great difficulty in making a satisfactory adjustment to the world of work and to the social system and is more likely to be an ineffective performer throughout his life.

We will not preempt our answers to whether prevention is possible beyond stressing the critical importance that every community must act to reduce the number of young people who currently reach adulthood unprepared educationally (and in other regards) to assume their economic and social responsibilities and roles. But we can add at this point that preventing school dropouts as well as preventing other forms of ineffective performance among adolescents is a challenge that must not be underestimated. Our society, like other developed societies, has opted to temporize rather than respond in strength. But it remains an open issue whether and to what extent more directed and intensive responses will prove effective.

Notes

1. Eli Ginzberg, Ethel L. Ginsburg, Dorothy L. Lynn, L. Mildred Vickers, and Sol W. Ginsburg, *The Unemployed: I. Interpretations; II. Case Studies* (New York: Harper & Brothers Publishers, 1943); and Eli Ginzberg, assisted by Joseph

Carwell, *The Labor Leader: An Exploratory Study* (New York: Macmillan Company, 1948).

2. Eli Ginzberg, Sol W. Ginsburg, Sidney Axelrad, and John L. Herma, *Occupational Choice: An Approach to a General Theory* (New York: Columbia University Press, 1951).

3. Eli Ginzberg and Douglas W. Bray, *The Uneducated* (New York: Columbia University Press, 1953); Eli Ginzberg, Sol W. Ginsburg, and John L. Herma, *Psychiatry and Military Manpower Policy—A Reappraisal of the Experience of World War II* (New York: Kings Crown Press, Columbia, 1953); Eli Ginzberg et al., *The Ineffective Soldier: Lessons for Management and the Nation*, Vol. I *The Lost Divisions*, Vol. II *Breakdown and Recovery*, Vol. III *Patterns of Performance* (New York: Columbia University Press, 1959).

4. Eli Ginzberg, with the assistance of James K. Anderson, Douglas W. Bray, and Robert W. Smuts, *The Negro Potential* (New York: Columbia University Press, 1956).

5. Eli Ginzberg, James K. Anderson, and John L. Herma, *The Optimistic Tradition and American Youth* (New York: Columbia University Press, 1962); Eli Ginzberg, ed., *The Nation's Children*, Vol. I *The Family and Social Change*, Vol. II *Development and Education*, Vol. III *Problems and Prospects* (New York: Columbia University Press, 1960); Eli Ginzberg, ed., *Values and Ideals of American Youth* (New York: Columbia University Press, 1961).

6. Eli Ginzberg, with Vincent Bryan, Grace T. Hamilton, John L. Herma, and Alice Yohalem, *The Middle-Class Negro in the White Man's World* (New York: Columbia University Press, 1967).

7. Eli Ginzberg, ed., *Employing the Unemployed* (New York: Basic Books, 1980); Eli Ginzberg, *The School/Work Nexus: Transition of Youth from School to Work* (Bloomington, Ind.: Phi Delta Kappa Educational Foundation, 1980).

8. Eli Ginzberg, Ivar E. Berg, Marcia K. Freedman, and John L. Herma, *The Social Order and Delinquency*, The Report of the President's Commission on Crime in the District of Columbia, Appendix Volume, 1966; Task Force on Individual Acts of Violence, National Commission on the Causes and Prevention of Violence, *Perspectives and Policies on Employment Problems of Youth and Juvenile Delinquency* (New York: Conservation of Human Resources, Columbia University, 1968); Eli Ginzberg and Dale L. Hiestand, *Mobility in the Negro Community* (Washington, D.C.: U.S. Commission on Civil Rights, Clearing House Publication, no. 11, 1968); The Twentieth Century Task Force on Employment Problems of Black Youth (Eli Ginzberg, chairman), *The Job Crisis for Black Youth* (New York: Praeger Publishers, 1971); *Manpower Advice for Government: Letters of the National Manpower Advisory Committee* (Washington, D.C.: U.S. Department of Labor, 1972); Eli Ginzberg and Robert M. Solow, eds., *The Great Society: Lessons for the Future* (New York: Basic Books, 1974); *Federal Manpower Policy in Transition, Letters of the National Manpower Advisory Committee* (Eli Ginzberg, chairman) (Washington, D.C.: U.S. Department of Labor, 1974); National Commission for Manpower Policy, *The First Five Years 1974–1979: A Report by Eli Ginzberg, chairman;* National Commission for Employment Policy (Eli Ginzberg, chairman), *Tell Me About Your School* (Washington, D.C.: 1979).

2

The Prevention Paradigm

The following points should be kept in mind in exploring the subject of preventing ineffective performance among young people and in attempting to extend the prevention paradigm from the health arena to social pathology.

- There has been little follow-up to Marc Lalonde's call (1973) for shifting health funding from therapeutics to prevention.[1]
- The U.S. Public Health Service's approach to prevention—setting targets and monitoring progress—has had some interim successes.
- The most important gains in health status appear to follow changes in life-styles, such as giving up smoking.
- AIDS is a potent reminder that with the passage of time new pathogens arise.
- Many forms of secondary or tertiary prevention are only partially successful because of noncompliance by individuals at risk.
- As Louise Russell has emphasized, many preventive approaches are cost increasing, not cost reducing, if one disregards the benefits of a longer (better quality) life.[2]
- A democratic society that values individual freedom often confronts the dilemma of balancing conflicting goals—in this case, better health versus individual freedom.

The thrust of these points for the analysis of preventive strategies to reduce ineffective performance among young people emphasizes the following:

- Even in the health arena, the potential of primary prevention is much reduced because most people in the United States live beyond age sixty-five.
- Secondary and tertiary prevention is costly and often fails because of motivational factors, namely, individual noncompliance.

• A democratic society is limited in raising resources for social interventions and in extensively using its police power.

In sum, there is no readily transferable paradigm from the health arena to social malfunctioning. How should our society conceptualize the challenge of reducing aberrant and ineffective performance?

Basic Institutions and the Developmental Process

Most young people pass from childhood and adolescence into adulthood without major difficulties. But a significant minority fail to make a satisfactory transition and enter their twenties seriously handicapped. The following institutions carry the principal responsibility for transforming the helpless infant into a performing adult: the nuclear family, the educational system, and the employing organization. Constantly interacting with these institutions are such potent secondary influences as neighborhood infrastructure, government policy and programs, the economy, and the changing value structure.

It should be noted that the analysis that follows does not include persons with developmental problems that result from genetic defects and/or severe disabilities.

Although the family has almost sole responsibility for nurturing infants and young children, its support often continues after the individual has reached adulthood. For example, many middle-class families assist their offspring with a down payment on a house. Access and articulation are characteristics of the developmental process in the sense that the child must be able to make the transition from family to school just as the high school or college dropout or graduate faces the challenge of finding and holding a job.

There is a corollary to the concept of the critical importance of developmental sequencing. Any serious shortcoming in an antecedent stage of development is likely to have adverse effects on the individual's opportunities in the next stage. If the adolescent finishes school without having effectively mastered the basic competences of reading, writing, and numerical skills, he or she may not be able to make a successful transition into the world of work, thereby encountering continuing difficulties in functioning as an adult.

The Nuclear Family

The family (or surrogate arrangement) has wide-ranging responsibilities for the newborn and the young child including ensuring that he or she makes steady progress along a series of axes—physical, intellectual, emotional, social—that will enable the youngster at age three, four, five, or six to make a smooth transition to nursery school, Headstart, kindergarten, or first grade. Most parents who have children for whom they have planned are generally able to discharge effectively their responsibilities for nurturing their offspring, although some children of affluent parents may also experience severe developmental problems.

The growing number of families headed by women increases the probability of developmental troubles. The rearing of a child or multiple children without the presence of the natural father or a stepfather carries additional vulnerability: the absence of a major wage earner; an inadequate amount of family income; excessive pressure on the mother's time and energy; welfare dependence; or any combination of these factors.

Sometimes these problems may be mitigated if mother and child are part of an extended family where relatives provide a range of supports. But such living arrangements are also frequently the source of tension and conflict, which can lead a mother and child to move out of a common household.

Further, the number of female-headed households fails to reflect the "risk factor" that a child will, for longer or shorter periods before its eighteenth birthday, be living in a family without two parents, natural or otherwise. And it also fails to take account of the number of children who are born out of wedlock and who grow up without any knowledge of, or relationship to, their natural father.

In sum, a significant number of children and adolescents are growing up in families that are poorly positioned to discharge their nurturing responsibilities. Although the proportion of "wanted children" has increased as a consequence of the use of birth control and abortion, and although the proportion of women in the labor force, including mothers with young children, is at an all-time high (over 50 percent in 1986), the proportion of female-headed households has also increased rapidly, and a significant minority of these families are solely dependent on welfare.

The Educational System

Most children begin school at age six, although a growing number between the ages of three and six are enrolled in nursery school and/ or kindergarten. This development reflects the confluence of two sets of forces: the growing belief among many child development specialists that it is advantageous for children between the ages of three and six to have some preschool experience; and the need of many working mothers to make arrangements for the supervision of their children during the hours that they work. In France, the state-supported Ecole Maternelle provides full-day activities for children from the age of two or three.

There is no agreement among child development specialists as to the critical age at which basic learning patterns are formed, but many believe that the first and second years of life are important. There is broad agreement, however, that depending on the stimulation and support received at home, children enter first grade better or worse prepared to cope with their early school experience. Children from low-income homes who have been in Headstart for one or two years are able to cope with the learning tasks in the first grade on more or less equal terms with children from more advantaged homes. What still remains moot is whether such an experience, unless reinforced, will have a lasting effect on their later performance.

There is growing recognition that for a host of reasons children entering first grade differ in their knowledge and learning readiness. This has led some educators to recommend that more flexibility be introduced into the first three years of school to enable young children to progress at their own rate.

Currently, big city school systems show marked variations in the tenth-, eleventh-, and twelfth-year reading (and other) scores of their pupils according to the income level of the neighborhood where the student lives. More to the point for our study, significant numbers of children do not read at grade level, and as time goes on many slip further behind. The poor readers, as they are advanced from grade to grade, encounter increasing difficulty in mastering the curriculum, and this is a potent factor in alienating them from their studies.

Several serious consequences ensue. Some students play hooky and spend more time on the streets than in the classroom. The students who fall behind are shunted to the least attractive junior and senior high schools. They have no prospect of being admitted to a specialized academic or vocational high school that selects its students on the basis of examinations or other criteria. After several more years of boring and unpleasant experiences in the classroom, these youths are prime candidates for early drop out.

The Employing Organization

Although a sixteen-year-old dropout who is reading at the sixth grade level, rather than at the tenth grade norm, may be able to pick up casual jobs and occasionally even a longer-term job, he or she will be excluded from securing a desirable beginning job, which offers training and promotion opportunities. Employers increasingly require at least a high school diploma for these positions. The vulnerability of this group of early dropouts, which in the case of minorities may account for 50 percent or more of the local cohort, is often compounded by other factors. For example, some of these young people early become involved in illicit and illegal activities, such as numbers running, buying and selling stolen merchandise, and drug trafficking, which may permanently distort their orientation and expectations regarding work and income. Some develop police records and others are sent away to reformatories. Some of the young women become pregnant, give birth out of wedlock, and consequently often drop out of school.

Developmental sequencing emphasizes the breakdowns in the rites of passage from school to work that afflict a significant proportion of young people who fail to obtain a high school diploma. Some may find the opportunity later on to remedy their lack of a diploma but most will remain permanently handicapped.

However, educational qualifications are by no means the only factors affecting the employability prospects of young people. The socialization of the young person and his or her orientation to the world of work, including an ability to meet the requirements of the employer, play a critical role. Also important is the help that the young person can elicit from family and friends in locating a desirable job opening, and whether or not he or she belongs to a minority group whose members continue to be discriminated against in the labor market.

These examples reflect the severity of handicaps with which some young people reach working age. Furthermore, a considerable number of youths from low-income households have been reared in families where the adults have had little or no regular attachment to the labor force, a condition further militating against socialization. In one of our earlier studies, we found students in junior and senior high schools in Harlem who had no personal knowledge of any individual who had earned a high school diploma and had succeeded in landing a regular job.[3]

In recent decades many young people have been attracted to non-conforming hairstyles and dress, which are viewed with disapproval by an overwhelming majority of employers. Unless the young person is counseled on how to dress and groom for a job interview, the game may be lost before it even begins. There is also a plethora of evidence that points to the difficulties that high school dropouts—and some graduates as well—have in filling out forms and coping with the other demands of the job application process.

One of the most important factors in a successful job search is who one knows and, equally important, who can pass on a friendly word to the individual responsible for hiring. The young person who has a large number of family members, friends, and acquaintances in the work world will be not one, but several, notches up on the youngster with few, if any, contacts with current job holders.

Although it is true that young people in their twenties have a considerably lower unemployment rate than teenagers, insufficient attention has been given to the predicament of many who fail to acquire an employment record during the early years after they leave school. If five years out of school, about age twenty-two or so, they have held only a few short-term jobs, employers will be wary about offering them a position. Their marginality in the labor market becomes more deeply etched with each passing year, for not only will prospective employers be skeptical about their lack of a regular employment record, but the applicant will not be able to show that he or she has acquired any significant body of skills.

The thrust of this schematic analysis of developmental sequencing highlights the fact that weaknesses in family structure are likely to be reflected in difficulties that young children encounter when they start school. If they fail to master the essentials, they fall behind. At some point they are likely to become alienated from the educational process and drop out. Without minimum competences—especially a reasonable level of literacy and work socialization—they will find it difficult and often impossible to secure a proper entrance job which would enable them to obtain training and to advance. They have been conditioned for ineffective adult performance.

Secondary Influences

In addition to the three principal developmental institutions—the family, school, and employers—we need to take account of several other potent forces that were previously identified—the neighborhood, government, the economy, and the value system.

Young children and particularly older children and adolescents are increasingly exposed to influences beyond the immediate family—the peers with whom they associate and the adults in their environment whose behavior signals what is valued and what is not. Neighborhoods, especially in large urban centers, which are often sharply differentiated by both income level and racial-ethnic composition, exercise important formative influences on youngsters who grow up within their boundaries.

Compare the neighborhood influences in an upper middle-class white suburb and those in a deteriorating inner-city area. The former points up for young people the opportunities available to adults who are well-educated and who pursue professional or managerial roles. In the slum it is the drug dealer, the prostitute, the numbers runner, and the racketeer who stand out. Doing well in school and gaining admission to an elite college is the goal of the suburbanite; widespread negativism toward school is characteristic of ghetto youth. The former come to see themselves as belonging to families that comprise the establishment; the latter are constantly reminded of their marginality. The summer camp, the country club, out-of-town trips, music and dancing lessons, and much more are part of the life of the affluent suburban child. The ghetto youngster has difficulty in finding an opportunity to shoot baskets or play softball.

Clearly, the passage from latency to adolescence and adulthood does not proceed free of stress or turmoil in the suburbs where drugs, alcoholism, depression, even suicide, occur with disturbing frequency. But it requires little imagination to note the differences between the two environments and to conclude that the affluent suburb is by far more favorable to the adolescent as he or she traverses the path to adulthood.

Many neoconservatives have criticized governmentally financed services, particularly welfare, as being dysfunctional to the people they are supposed to help—the nonworking poor. One need not be a neoconservative to acknowledge that growing up in a family that remains on welfare for long periods of time is likely to be a stunting experience. The thrust of neoconservative criticism, however, should be directed not to the elimination of welfare but rather to the need for reforms to help families escape from welfare.

But welfare is only one of a wide range of public services. When one considers the quantity and quality of other governmental services available to the poor and the affluent it quickly becomes clear that the advantages are largely with the latter. Think for a moment of the per capita expenditures for public education; the maintenance of roads, parks, and other public places; sanitation; police protection; access to health services; and much more. All of these services are much better in affluent than in low-income neighborhoods.

Another critical parameter is the behavior of the economy, particularly the state of the job market. The ability of young people to make a satisfactory transition from school to work depends in no small measure on the local labor market. Although the U.S. economy has been able to create a great many new jobs over the last decade and a half, this achievement has gone hand in hand with a persistently high level of unemployment among minority youth. The U.S. economy has not operated at full employment since the latter part of World War II, which means that some people, particularly those with few competences and skills, will be at the end of the queue and suffer from long spells of unemployment. Minority youth who have dropped out of school have been and continue to be the most vulnerable group when it comes to finding and holding a regular job.

Some analysts believe that now that the baby boom generation has passed into adulthood, the reduced number of new entrants into the labor force will make it easier for all young people to make the transition into the job market. There is some supporting evidence for this view from the state of Massachusetts, which has enjoyed a tight labor market over the last few years. But other regions of the country are not likely soon to match the economic expansion of New England, and even if they do, there is no certainty that poorly prepared youths will get regular jobs.

The last macro-factor that impacts the developmental process is the basic value structure, particularly the attitudes of the dominant population toward racial and ethnic minorities. It is hard to exaggerate the invidiousness of racial prejudice on the attitudes and behavior of successive generations of blacks, including the youngsters who are currently growing up. Although the country has made considerable progress since World War II in expanding opportunities for blacks and in accepting those who are able to cope, racism continues to threaten the development of many who are both black and poor. Many grow up with little self-esteem, with latent aggressions, with underdeveloped ambitions and goals, and with a deep sense of injury, which leads them to believe that no matter how hard they try, it will be to no avail because whites are in the seats of power and will not deal fairly with them. Why bother to make the effort? Our society, however, expects the individual to do his or her best and to assume primary responsibility for changing his or her life chances—hence the destructiveness of a response when racism undermines effort.

The foregoing analysis has sought to make clear two central points that are at the heart of adult ineffectiveness. The first is the critical role of developmental sequencing as the child moves from family to school into the work arena. The second is the potent influence of selected environmental factors on the developmental process, in particular the neighborhood, government services, economic trends, and the value system. Any serious effort at preventing adult ineffectiveness must not only take account of the developmental process but also the powerful influence of these environmental forces.

Changing Strategies of Intervention

During the 1930s, the period of the New Deal, the nation experienced a radical turning point in dealing with ineffective performance, including efforts directed to reducing it through the introduction of early intervention devices. The easiest way to put the New Deal into historical context is to set out briefly the major approaches that had been institutionalized prior to the 1930s and to contrast them with the Rooseveltian reforms.

In the first three decades of this century widespread ineffectiveness was concentrated among three groups: the urban poor of the nation's large cities, who for the most part consisted of immigrant families and their first-generation descendants; a considerable minority of Americans of native-born parentage who had migrated from farm areas to the city in search of industrial employment, some of whom encountered difficulties in making a successful transition; and blacks, over 80 percent of whom were still living in the South, predominantly as tenant farmers on land that was losing its productivity. The special situation of the blacks aside, the urban poor suffered from the four "Ds"—destitution, disease, desertion, and premature death.

How did our society intervene to make a person's life chances a little better? Oversimplified, one can identify the following principal intervention devices:

- Major public health rules and regulations were promulgated and enforced to reduce or eliminate some of the more egregious sources of disease and premature death.
- Public sector action also was taken to protect children and young people by raising the working age and restricting the hours that they were permitted to work; similar protective legislation was enacted for women.
- The number of years that a young person was required to attend school and the length of the school year were increased, as were the resources available to operate the public education system.
- Safety in the workplace was improved; trade unions succeeded in reducing work hours and improving wages and benefits.

Philanthropy and social welfare organizations directed many of their efforts to the following:

- The discovery and eradication of major disease entities such as pellagra.
- The funding and staffing of clinics and hospitals that provided a considerable amount of free services to the poor.
- The operation of orphanages to help raise the children of broken families when the surviving parent could not cope or when both parents had died and no relatives were able or willing to assume the responsibility.

- The establishment and operation in or close to low-income neighborhoods of settlement houses that provided an oasis where young people could enjoy athletic, cultural, artistic, and recreational activities.
- The financing of scholarship and fellowship programs for talented young people to enable them to attend college or to develop their musical or other artistic talents.
- The development of special language and citizenship programs aimed specifically at speeding the acculturation of immigrants, particularly those who came from non-English-speaking backgrounds.

Important as these governmental and philanthropic programs were in improving the conditions of life and the career prospects of the poor and their children, it would be a mistake to see them as having had more than modest leverage. The dominant realities were determined by the skill, competence, and energy of the individual family, primarily the male head of household, to gain a place on the occupational ladder and to advance up that ladder to a point where his earnings could cover the basic needs, and more, of those for whom he was responsible. To the extent that many heads of households for a shorter or longer period were unable to meet this challenge, or in the event of their premature death or desertion, the principal intervening institutions included relatives who were able and willing to assist; community self-help organizations (Landsmannschaften, etc.), which advanced credit, served as an employment network, and provided a host of other supports; and the local priest who through leverage on his more well-to-do members and through his connections with the local political club could help find jobs for heads of households and/or their children when they came of working age. The local political club that had a pool of short- and long-term jobs to distribute among its more active members or those whom they recommended also helped.

These facts suggest that the principal cause of poverty and destitution was the failure of the male head of household to find and hold a full-time job. When that happened, relatives, friends, and communal institutions bestirred themselves on behalf of the unemployed father to find him a job, or when that was not possible, to assist his spouse and adolescent children to find opportunities to earn money.

Two further observations: In the case of native-born migrants who left the farm to seek work in industry many, when they ran into hard times (especially after 1929), picked themselves up and returned to the family homestead. Second, special attention must be directed to the circumstances of the blacks who, as noted above, were overwhelmingly living in the South as tenant farmers, largely out of sight and out of mind of the rest of the country, except in the event of an egregious incident such as Scottsboro (1932). The majority of the black population was uneducated or poorly educated and suffered from malnutrition. Adult males were barred from all but the most disagreeable types of nonfarm jobs, and their wives who worked in white homes helped to keep the family afloat, but just barely, through "toting" and a few dollars of cash earnings.

If one agrees that this is a fair summary of the conditions affecting most blacks as late as 1940, there are two alternative assessments of the disproportionate number of severely disadvantaged blacks in 1986. One view would stress the large numbers of blacks whose condition is much improved by virtue of their broadened access to the U.S. opportunity structure. The other would emphasize the persistent marginality of many blacks as reflected in the disproportionately large number of teenagers who give birth out of wedlock; high rates of school leaving; drug addiction; death by homicide; crime; unemployment; withdrawal from the labor force; welfare dependency; and still other symptoms of a high degree of social malfunctioning.

Questions have often been raised about the reasons for the differences in the upward mobility of immigrant groups and blacks. Aside from the validity of the observation—it took the Boston Irish five generations before one of them won the presidency and it took Italian-Americans almost as long before one of them won a place on the Supreme Court—the critical fact is that blacks have lacked the support of two potent intermediaries of an earlier day—the Catholic Church and the local political club.

But to return to the main line of analysis. The New Deal reforms responded to the following:

- The inability of families and philanthropy to meet the income needs of men and their dependents facing long periods of unemployment during the Great Depression. Accordingly, the need for the transfer of income from taxpayers to the poor by the government was accepted for the first time.
- The New Deal reforms also recognized for the first time that the federal government should take an active role to generate public sector jobs when the private sector was clearly unable to provide employment opportunities for all who wanted and needed to work.
- Innovative programs under the aegis of the federal government were directed to assisting youth from low-income families to remain in school (work-study programs). In the event that they were no longer in school, youths could enroll in the Civilian Conservation Corps

for the purpose of engaging in worthwhile environmental projects (national parks), which paid a modest stipend, 80 percent of which was sent home to assist their families.

- The New Deal also established two insurance systems—old age and survivors insurance, and unemployment insurance—aimed at providing minimum income to older persons and their survivors, and to the short-term unemployed and their families.
- Aid to Families with Dependent Children (AFDC), a federal welfare program, was enacted, which assisted and encouraged women with minor children to stay at home to rear them when the husband died or could not work, and thereby avoid the breakup of the family.
- In a number of states with strong trade unions, legislators moved to raise the school-leaving age to reduce the competition for scarce jobs between experienced male heads of household and adolescents first entering the labor market.

If one jumps ahead thirty years to the mid-1960s when the Great Society programs were being implemented, the following were the principal axes of reform:

- The affirmation of a federal responsibility for skill training to improve employability, first enunciated by the passage of the Manpower Development and Training Act (MDTA) of 1962.
- The establishment of the Job Corps in 1964 as a substitute for a much broader youth conservation corps that Senator Hubert Humphrey fought for but failed to get passed. The Job Corps centers were aimed at providing second-chance opportunities for the most seriously disadvantaged young people who lacked both educational competences and job skills.
- The establishment of opportunities for members of low-income communities under the antipoverty legislation of 1964 to play an active role (maximum feasible participation) in the design and implementation of various federally funded programs.
- The Civil Rights Act of 1964.
- Medicare and Medicaid (1965). The latter was aimed at expanding access to health care services, particularly for mothers and children on AFDC, and for other persons living at or close to the poverty level.
- The Education Act of 1965, which provided federal funds for schools that had differentially large numbers of children from disadvantaged homes.

- Special adjustments in the armed forces' selection criteria by the Department of Defense, according to an agreement between the White House and the Pentagon, which enabled about a quarter million special servicemen to be inducted.
- The appropriation by Congress of sizable sums for urban housing and urban renewal, much of it aimed at the rehabilitation of low-income neighborhoods.
- The enactment of a number of additional programs, such as Headstart, to respond to the special problems of poor families, especially their inability to pay tuition for their children in nursery school.

Although these items do not constitute an inclusive list of the many new departures that characterized the ambitious and far-flung efforts of the Great Society programs to eliminate poverty in the United States, we have attempted to enumerate the more important pieces of legislation that were enacted.

We are now in a better position to identify and assess the principal forms of federal intervention (usually in association with the states) over the last half-century that were aimed at improving the developmental experiences and life chances of children and young people. These measures are discussed below.

- Cash income (welfare) was provided to families headed by women with minor children. Because this was a shared program between the federal government and the states, and many states (mostly in the South) failed to appropriate the full amount of the mandated matching grants, the monthly payments were often very small and were further eroded by the inflation subsequent to 1965. However, the substantial expansion of the Food Stamp program in the 1970s resulted in significant additional in-kind relief.
- Under Title XX of the Social Security Act, the federal government made funds available to the states to provide support services for low-income families, such as enabling them to obtain child care free or below cost. This allowed some mothers on welfare to go to work.
- The Headstart program was unique in the sense that it was designed specifically to help the children of low-income families overcome some of their specific developmental handicaps, resulting from lack of stimulation and early learning opportunities.
- The evaluations of Title I and Title II of the Education Act of 1965 point to modest gains, but even the most enthusiastic advocates of such intervention do not claim that the federal funds have been

able to equalize the educational experience of children from seriously disadvantaged homes and those from middle-class homes.

- As for Medicaid, the weight of the evidence is that its passage did broaden and deepen the access of children on AFDC to health care services even though the health status of their families remained several notches below those higher on the income scale.
- There is no simple assessment of the impact on youth of the panoply of training programs (MDTA and the Comprehensive Employment and Training Act or CETA), which for the 1962 to 1981 period involved total expenditures (adult and youth) of approximately $100 billion. What the studies point up is that the residential Job Corps Centers, which provided second-chance opportunities for the most severely disadvantaged youth, did well for those who stayed the course. The per-year cost was in the $10,000 to $12,000 range. The summer training programs and other training programs provided varying degrees of work experience, socialization, and modest skill acquisition. They provided many needy youth with income, but only small numbers were able to find a regular job as a result of their training.
- Although the Department of Defense did not publicize the outcome of its large-scale induction of special servicemen, the follow-up data provide unequivocal evidence that the vast majority, some nine out of ten, performed satisfactorily or better.
- Many of the poor who became engaged in the political process or in supervisory roles as a result of the antipoverty programs gained experience on which they were later able to build a career.

In sum, most of the programs were adult-, not youth-oriented. The strengthening of the family never went much beyond minimum welfare payments for AFDC, which were more for maintenance than for rehabilitation. Headstart had the quality of a "preventive" program in the sense that it aimed to prevent children from low-income homes from entering school with learning handicaps. The Job Corps was the most conspicuous type of "second-chance" opportunity program.

With the advantage of hindsight, one can argue that the New Deal, except for Social Security, was primarily a short-term response to the overwhelming problems engendered by the collapse of the private economy, compared to the Great Society, which represented a heroic amalgam of programs aimed at eliminating the barriers to equality of opportunity in American life across the entire spectrum, from civil rights to access to health care. The shortcomings of the Johnson reforms were rooted in an underestimation of the difficulties and costs involved in structural change, the lack of broad public support, and the preemption of tax dollars by the Vietnam War.

There is another moral that can be extracted from this reconstruction. The three most potent forces contributing to improved opportunities for disadvantaged groups were the strong performance of the U.S. economy since 1940, especially its job-generating potential; the lowering of financial barriers to higher education; and the much improved, if still unsatisfactory, arena of race relations. If one accepts these statements, then it follows that the federal and state governments may have been more successful in contributing to the well-being of the disadvantaged population through the improvement of the macroeconomic and social environment than they have been in their more focused efforts at direct assistance to the poor.

The analysis, thus far, has been heavily centered on the role of the public sector and understandably so, as government has been the principal agent for societal intervention during the past half-century. However, the activities of the nonprofit sector must also be considered because of its continuing role in seeking constructive change, much of it directed to assisting a wide array of disadvantaged groups.

In the pre–New Deal days, the nonprofit sector made important contributions to the urban poor, as noted earlier, by providing short-term financial assistance to families in need; reinforcing through community organizations the dominant value system of self-reliance, work, and responsibility; providing educational and cultural opportunities and health services; and assisting in finding jobs for those who needed to work. Once government began to take over the income maintenance function in 1933, most social welfare organizations shifted focus and under the stimulus of a professional staff became more involved in providing social casework and psychiatric services to troubled families. Moreover, with time they came to be government contractors providing a wide range of services to clients for whom government paid most or all of the bill, such as child guidance, family placement and supervision, health care, and much more.

What have been the links and interactions between nonprofit institutions and the key aspects of the lives of the poor and disadvantaged in terms of early development, school, neighborhood, adolescence, and work? Although most large public educational systems have failed to provide a satisfactory educational experience for large numbers of children from low-income homes, there have been relatively few voluntary organizations that have succeeded in exerting a constructive influence on this complex system. There are many instances of beneficial interventions, from special tutoring provided by volunteers to donations of outside funds to support athletics and other special projects. But only rarely has a nonprofit organization been able to make a significant impact on the effectiveness of a ghetto school through close cooperation.

However, private schools, particularly parochial schools, have made important contributions by opening themselves to all races, thereby providing many black and Hispanic families with an opportunity to send their children to a school that generally offers a better quality developmental experience than they would find in their local public school.

There is a limited amount of voluntary support provided poor families by organizations that arrange for children from low-income homes to go away for a fortnight or so to summer camp; to be taken by a concerned adult on Saturdays to visit different parts of the city; and to be afforded similar opportunities from time to time to escape from their narrowly confined boundaries. But such interventions are limited in number and scope, in part because of the relatively small number of affluent blacks who volunteer and the reluctance of most whites to cross the color line.

Adolescence is a period of turmoil and stress—what is euphemistically called "acting out." Although the progress on the civil rights front over the last quarter-century may have contributed greatly to the normalization of adolescent experience among middle-class blacks by delineating channels that, if followed, will lead to a career and social progress, the plight of the poor and disadvantaged black has probably worsened because of the widening gap between expectation and reality. There is good reason to postulate that the growing menace of the drug culture, teenage out-of-wedlock pregnancy, and the appallingly high rate of homicide among black males mask in considerable measure the unrelieved aggression resulting from desires deferred and thwarted.

In sum, this schematic review of the principal intervention devices that our society has used to improve the development and life chances of poor and disadvantaged children and youth over the past half-century emphasizes the following:

- The assumption of responsibility by government, in a federal-state joint program, to provide minimum income for female-headed households with minor children.
- The establishment of a large-scale Food Stamp Program that enables the poor and the near-poor to purchase food at subsidized prices, which, in fact, has become a broad income support program.
- Access of children on AFDC and other selected poor families to broadened and deepened health care services (Medicaid and other federal-state programs).

- State and locally supported programs that have made graduation from high school the national norm, and with assistance from the federal government, have removed most of the financial barriers keeping young people from enrolling in college.
- A limited amount of special assistance to preschool children in low-income families to facilitate the employment of their mothers (child care), and to provide young children with a stimulating preschool experience (Headstart). Also, special federal funding to provide additional resources for new and enriched programs in public schools with large numbers of disadvantaged children.
- The establishment and operation of a range of family and individual counseling and mental health services for families and children in need of psychological support and guidance.
- Child placement programs for younger and older children who cannot continue to live in their natural family because of death, illness, or emotional conflict.
- The availability of family planning information and counseling, free contraceptives, sex education, and abortion services for adolescents.
- A limited number of rehabilitative programs for young people who need detoxification services and for previously institutionalized youth offenders who are reentering civilian society.
- Alternative or second-chance schooling, such as a general equivalency diploma (GED), for young people who are unable to cope with the conventional high school.
- A wide variety of training, employment, and work experience programs, including residential Job Corps centers, to improve the competences and skills of young people who face serious difficulties in making the transition into the world of work.
- A large variety of philanthropically supported local service programs directed at children and young people from disadvantaged homes, which span the range from "fresh air" vacations in the summer to special scholarship aid for superior students.
- The lowering of discriminatory barriers, especially those based on race, ethnicity, and income, through broadened opportunities for disadvantaged families to enroll their children in parochial schools.

We conclude this section with a few observations about the foregoing major interventions that have dominated the political-social arena during the past half-century. The family and societal ills to which these interventions have been addressed have not remained static over this long period of time. Effective intervention programs must be constantly reassessed to determine whether they are responsive to the emergence of new conditions such as the earlier onset of sexual activity.

Once the target population requiring assistance is broadly defined, such as the poor and the near-poor, only governmental budgets are large enough to be able to finance significant programs. Moreover, even governmental programs are seldom financed at a level that can respond to more than a part of the needy population.

In our federal-state-local governmental structure, the quality of governmental programming, especially service programs, depends heavily on the effectiveness of different levels of the bureaucracy and on the coordination among them. It depends as well on the coordination between nonprofit or for-profit providers and government.

The operation of a major intervention program such as AFDC is almost certain over time to alter in varying degrees the attitudes and behavior of individuals who use it or may contemplate using it, and also to lead to changes in the attitudes of the community at large toward the program.

The U.S. experience over the last half-century has provided unequivocal evidence that the tax-paying public resists providing funds for major efforts to prevent social pathology and to rehabilitate disadvantaged families and their children, even though it will support a wide range of government programs to provide minimum maintenance grants once people are in trouble.

These considerations frame the exploration that follows, which centers on assessing alternative strategies of intervention.

Prevention and Other Intervention Strategies

There is broad agreement among theoreticians and practitioners that the multiple interventions of both the New Deal and the Great Society programs have not provided the sought-for answers as to how our society can reduce and eliminate widespread ineffective behavior, which is characteristic of so many adolescents and young adults. Some believe that the broad ameliorative governmental programs of income transfer, family support, educational reform, employment and training programs, and still other measures have simply been on too small a scale to help the large numbers of disadvantaged families whose children and youth are in need of special assistance. A counterview holds that many or most of the governmental programs have led to dysfunctional outcomes by sending the poor the wrong signals, which in turn have led them to adopt attitudes and behavior that have contributed to their ineffective performance and long-term entrapment at the bottom of the social scale. In the present context, there is little to be gained from a close examination of these sharply conflicting explanatory theories. Both sides agree that a great amount of ineffective behavior continues, and it is this overriding phenomenon that must be addressed.

To provide a focus for our exploration of alternative intervention strategies, we define below six major types of dysfunctional behavior characteristic of adolescents and young adults.

1. Dropping out of school without having acquired a high school diploma and without possessing an acceptable level of functional literacy is prelude to continuing ineffectiveness. While more than four out of every five adolescents earn a high school diploma, and in affluent suburbs the proportion is nine out of ten or even higher, the average for Hispanic and black groups in inner-city low-income neighborhoods is in the 40 to 60 percent range.

2. A significant number of teenagers, particularly blacks, have one or more children out of wedlock, and as a result many fail to complete their education and prematurely confront child-rearing responsibilities and other challenges with which they are not prepared to cope.

3. Largely as a consequence of early motherhood, many young women are forced to go on the welfare rolls to assure themselves and their child the basic necessities of life. But once on welfare, many adapt to their status because of their lack of employment skills.

4. Although the trafficking in and the use of drugs are not bounded by neighborhood or class but are a danger to all adolescents, such involvement represents a special threat to inner-city youth with their more limited career opportunities and constricted life goals.

5. About the most telling evidence of the serious malfunctioning in the developmental experiences of young black males is the appalling homicide rate, 66.8 per 100,000, which accounts for 43 percent of all deaths among those aged fifteen to twenty-four years.

6. The sixth and last manifestation of ineffective performance relates to the large number of high school dropouts who enter their twenties without having acquired much by way of work experience or occupational skills and who become only marginally attached to the work force, interspersing short-term job holding with recurrent bouts of unemployment.

As the next step in the development of an intervention schema, we have identified the following four axes (see Figure 2.1): specific programs, process improvements, macro-changes, and second-chance opportunities. These categories tend to spill over, as for instance when a school system broadens the choices available to graduates of junior high school with respect to the senior high schools to which they have access. From one perspective, the broadening of choice can be viewed as a specific type of program intervention aimed at reducing later dropouts and adding to the competences of school-leavers and graduates. But to the extent

FIGURE 2.1
Behavior-Intervention Matrix

	School Dropouts	Teenage Pregnancy	Welfare Status	Drug Addicts	Homicide Victims	Marginal Labor Force Role
Specific Programs						
Process Improvements						
Macro-Changes						
Second-Chance Opportunities						

that the specific program is successful, it can be viewed as process improvement in the developmental sequencing.

To elaborate further, many societal interventions are programmatic in that they add something new to or alter the relationships among parts of the extant system, as for instance increasing the number of truancy officers to check with families on the unexplained absences of their children from school; the establishment or expansion/improvement of service programs aimed at helping drug addicts or pregnant teenagers to cope with their current problems and assisting them in restructuring their future behavior (process intervention).

Changes aimed at strengthening the developmental process in the social arena have many of the characteristics of the prevention paradigm in the health sector. They would require interventions that significantly improve the opportunities of families, the schools, and businesses and institutions to meet more effectively the sequential needs of children, adolescents, and young adults, and thereby help to prevent ineffective performance in the future.

But there is nothing easy about successful process interventions. It is very difficult for society to intervene to compensate for a missing parent, ineffective parents, and other major shortcomings in the family structure that are likely to have deleterious effects on a child's development. Experience has taught that removing the child from a malfunctioning home is no assurance of a better outcome. A similar cautionary view must be taken of society's potential to bring about within a reasonable span of time a significant improvement in the functioning of ghetto schools.

While such process improvements generally require more resources, the availability of additional resources has not sufficed to accomplish many essential reforms. Public education has demonstrated only limited capacity to improve its performance to ensure that most adolescents in the inner city complete their schooling in possession of an acceptable level of functional literacy.

We argued earlier that the macro-change reflected in rapid job increases contributed significantly to improving the circumstances of many poor people in the post–World War II era. In the context of the present discussion of process interventions, we need to look more closely at the civil rights–affirmative action efforts since the passage of the Civil Rights Act of 1964, in order to assess its contribution to the reduction of ineffective performance among the oncoming generation of youth and young adults.

The conventional interpretation emphasizes that arbitrary forms of discrimination distort the attitudes and behavior of young people during their developmental years. Therefore, the lowering and removal of discriminatory barriers must be seen as a significant contribution to reducing ineffectiveness, surely in the long term.

But in the short and middle term, serious problems persist. Consider the gap that has arisen in the minds of many young blacks between the high expectations that the promise of the civil rights movement engendered and the overwhelming evidence that their own circumstances have not noticeably improved. One can point to the weakening of the ghetto leadership that followed upon the out-migration of successful blacks who were able to take advantage of the favorable by-products of desegregation. And with the advantage of hindsight, one can also point to the disproportionate deflection and diffusion of energy by leaders in ghetto communities that pursued legal remedies based on busing to improve their schools. Even so potent a macro-intervention as the civil rights revolution does not necessarily lead to beneficial outcomes for all or most of the previously disadvantaged, surely not in the short and middle term.

The last category of interventions designed to reduce ineffective behavior among adolescents and young adults has been identified as second-chance opportunities, which often, but not always, involve exposing them to radically different environments. A few preliminary observations about this strategically important intervention device are in order. First, we must emphasize that the important transition from school to work, which all adolescents confront, carries with it the promise of a second chance. Regrettably that was more true in the past than at present or than it is likely to be in the future. In generations past, a person's performance in school had only minor bearing on whether the individual could get a job and, except for the professions, was not closely related to future career opportunities and advancement. Today and tomorrow, the individual's educational achievement is and will be of much greater importance in determining his or her place in the labor market.

Another aspect of second chance built into the developmental cycle was the role of marriage and motherhood that offered many young women the prospect of a break with their earlier life.

A third example, of considerable importance in the 1940 to 1970 period, was the proportion of young men who enlisted or were inducted into one of the armed forces. The two-three-four year initial term of service placed all of them in a vastly different environment from the one to which they had been accustomed. Although a significant minority could not cope, the vast majority were able to earn an honorable discharge, which for war veterans carried many valuable postmilitary benefits (GI bill).

Having detailed these schematic differentiations among intervention devices aimed at reducing ineffective performance or increasing effective performance, we are in a position to establish and deploy a matrix in Figure 2.1 in which the principal sources of ineffective behavior among adolescents and young adults are viewed from the perspective of the four principal types of intervention devices.

The notations that follow are chiefly suggestive and make no pretense of treating the subject in depth. They suggest how the matrix can be used to guide policy and programs aimed at reducing ineffectiveness among adolescents and young adults.

School Dropouts

There is no need to denigrate the possible constructive outcome of specific program interventions by raising questions about their overall effectiveness, namely, affording students who fail an opportunity to go to summer school to make up for their failure; providing high school students from low-income homes with an opportunity for part-time jobs to enlarge their horizons and provide them with some discretionary income; the improved "holding power" of some alternative schools; and so forth.

The primary reasons for dropping out prior to graduation from high school must be embedded in the following: serious retardation in learning skills (often two or more years); boredom with what goes on in the classroom; lack of understanding of the value of a diploma for later job and career prospects; absence of family encouragement to complete high school; and the lure of the street and one's peers.

If these points reasonably identify some of the more potent factors contributing to dropping out, it follows that no specific intervention program is likely, on its own, to have more than a marginal effect, if that. What is called for and what should be more or less evident is the need for process interventions that would make the prior schooling experience of the potential dropouts more meaningful and productive, and an appreciation on the part of these young people that the completion of high school and the acquisition of basic competences would yield them large returns in the years to come.

Short of the schools being able to meet the test of effectively teaching these youngsters, and short of the demonstrated effect that a high school diploma will in fact pay off for them, it is difficult to see how the dropout rate can be significantly reduced.

This last finding emphasizes the importance of second-chance opportunities. The young adult of nineteen or twenty differs, usually greatly, from the early adolescent of fourteen or fifteen. The differences are in part the result of the maturation process itself and in part reflect the wider range of knowledge and experience of the young adult. Many youngsters, who at fourteen "know" that school doesn't count, may at twenty have reevaluated themselves and the world in which they must make their way and come to believe that school does count. Accordingly, some would welcome a second-chance opportunity to remedy their educational deficiencies.

Teenage Pregnancy

Those who have been actively involved in helping teenagers who are pregnant have often been frustrated by the complex individual and societal problems that they encounter. To mention a few: parental views about abortion; the attitude of the putative father; the conflicting desires of the young mother; the absence of an array of support programs that would assist the young mother to have her child and still continue her own development.

There are a large number of specific programs, in particular family planning agencies, that provide sex counseling and birth control information and devices for adolescents, especially young women. Along with arranging for abortions, these programs can be seen as preventing births among teenagers who become pregnant and preventing pregnancies among the large number who engage in early and continuing sexual activity. It is far from clear what the complex of forces are that lead some teenagers, some as young as fourteen, to decide to have their baby, and it is even more difficult to identify the reasons that many who have one child decide after a relatively short time to have another. A few of the factors that probably are important in this not well-understood decisionmaking process include family and community tolerance of births out of wedlock; the knowledge that mother and child can obtain welfare; and the demonstrated effect that many teenagers who have had a child are not demonstrably worse off.

If one postulates, as one must, that teenagers who become pregnant and decide to have a child are making an important if implicit judgment about the quality of their early life as well as their prospects for the future, then any significant reduction in out-of-wedlock births would have to address the potential of "process interventions" that alone hold the prospect of altering the life chances of these adolescents from seriously depressed backgrounds. Oversimplified, once they become pregnant, early motherhood appears to offer an escape from an existence that provides little in the form of satisfaction and love and holds little promise of becoming more attractive and rewarding in the future. If society is seriously concerned about the reduction and elimination of teenage pregnancy and early motherhood, it faces the formidable challenge of intervening early, strongly, and continuously in the development process to provide realistic alternative outcomes for these disadvantaged youngsters. In the absence of preferred alternatives the problem is not likely to diminish.

There are macro-reforms underway that may contribute to its reduction, such as the willingness of some communities and school systems to broaden access to sex education and birth control techniques. An increasing number of black leaders have begun to speak out forcibly about seeking to alter the attitudes and behavior of the black community so that it becomes less indulgent of teenage out-of-wedlock births. These reforms can probably help to reverse the trend but it is doubtful that even the two, working together, will be able, in the absence of new interventions, to reduce significantly the numbers of out-of-wedlock teenage births.

Accordingly, second-chance opportunities are needed to encourage young mothers to complete their schooling, at least to obtain a high school diploma or its equivalent; to be assisted in finding a job; to have access to child care facilities; and to retain interim access to important public services such as Medicaid, until their earnings enable them to leave the welfare rolls. The sheer enumeration of these basic services to which they need access is a powerful reminder of the great difficulties that our society faces in helping teenage mothers to enter the mainstream. Clearly, preventing their having a child while in their teens would be a preferred alternative.

Welfare Status

A major source of new applications/acceptances on welfare rolls is the young teenage mother who, in the absence of a wage-earning male, frequently has no other source of income to cover living expenses for her child and herself. Although many adults who go onto the rolls leave within a relatively brief time (less than two years), many teenage mothers remain for a decade if not longer.

Many states have initiated workfare programs, with the objective of speeding the departure from the welfare rolls of men and women who are deemed to be employable and who have no children under six who require their continuing attention. While the early evidence from these experimental programs tends to be favorable in the sense that the costs of operating them are more than covered by reductions in welfare expenditures and/or gains in employment and income by the former welfare clients, these results speak more to short-run than to long-run gains. The latter have still to be demonstrated.

Because early motherhood and the lack of employability are closely linked to prior poor developmental opportunities, the long-term reduction of the welfare rolls would have to look to process interventions. But important as process interventions would be to achieve a long-term reduction in the welfare population, they would not suffice. Macro-interventions would also be needed, especially in periods with cyclically high rates of unemployment and underemployment. A society that directed its efforts only to strengthening the work skills of the population, important as that effort would be, would also need some type of public job creation to ensure an adequate level of demand for those who want and need to work.

Because of the inherent limitations of each of the above interventions, there is need for a "second-chance" approach that would help some part of the welfare clientele to overcome their handicaps to employment by offering opportunities for educational remediation, skill training, employment support services (child care), and, on occasion, a prosthesis or other medical rehabilitation.

Drug Addicts

There has been growing concern these past years with the increasing exposure of adolescents to the drug culture and particularly the dangers of such exposure for youth growing up in the ghetto where trafficking in drugs has not been a prime target of the police and where parents are poorly positioned to assume an active role in fighting its extension. The epidemic-like spread of crack has led some informed observers to warn that the dangers of the recent past are being multiplied and remultiplied by the spread of this most insidious form of cocaine.

On the programmatic front, there have been educational programs that have sought to prevent/delay the use of drugs by teenagers. The evaluative studies point to some, but no overwhelming, successes even as these programs have become more sophisticated in design and execution. A growing number of programs have also been put in place that address the problems of young people who want to kick the habit; again these show some, but no overwhelmingly positive results.

These findings should come as no surprise considering the fact that while many youngsters experiment with taking drugs, only a minority become addicted and move from less to more dangerous substance abuse. The minority that gets hooked consists to a large degree of young people who, lacking immediate satisfactions and seeing few prospects for a better future, seek the surcease that steady drug use can provide.

As modern open societies find it difficult to interdict the inflow of dangerous drugs, it does not follow that they cannot devise better control measures than they have to reduce, if not eliminate, the scourge. Lifetime sentences for previously convicted drug dealers and widespread examinations of employees for drug use may not be the answer, but more and better control measures should be explored.

Although second-chance programs aimed at the rehabilitation of former drug addicts have proved at best only moderately successful, one must be careful, just as in the case of macro-interventions, not to write them off. At a minimum, there is need for enlarged and improved rehabilitation services to make it easier for those who seek to overcome their addiction to enter and pursue a normal life of self-supporting work.

Homicide Victims

The most difficult of all challenges presented by aberrant behavior among late adolescents and young adults is found among black males, whose rate of death from homicide, 66.8 per 100,000, far exceeds that of the general population. In terms of loss of years of potential life, homicide ranks first among black males, far in advance of any other cause. When one considers the individual and social losses entailed by this high homicide rate, one cannot help being surprised as to how little attention has been directed to analyzing its causes and exploring solutions.

On the programmatic front, Congress has from time to time addressed the issue of tighter control of guns, the principal lethal weapons in homicide, but the opposition lobby has been consistently powerful enough to beat back efforts to limit their sale. State and local ordinances have been passed that raise the penalties for possession of a gun without a permit, but, as the homicide data underscore, these efforts have not sufficed to prevent persons who are determined to secure weapons from doing so. What the laws have done is to raise the price.

The broad-scale possession of guns among many black males stems in part from the considerable number who are engaged, regularly or intermittently, in illegal activities, particularly armed robbery. The gun is one of the tools of the trade. In the event that they are attacked, threatened, cheated, get into a fight, feel insulted, or are otherwise challenged, carrying a gun makes it more likely that they will use it if and when they find themselves under stress.

It does not follow, of course, that more stringent rules about the purchase of guns and their effective enforcement would bring an end to homicides, many of which, even now, result from the use of other lethal weapons such as knives. But tougher controls should lead to substantial declines in unpremeditated deaths.

The question arises why so many young black males own guns and are prone to use them. The answers are close at hand. Many are reared in an environment where crime and the taking of life are almost routine occurrences and where the police often close their eyes to what is going on. Many young black men believe that society is rigged against them and will not give them any sort of break. Their pent-up aggression increases with the passage of every year. These and related developmental experiences turn many young blacks into a tinderbox ready to explode. A significant reduction in their homicide rate would require significant changes in their developmental experiences. Only macro-interventions that showed these ghetto males that our society has a place for them and needs and wants them could help to moderate the buildup of aggression, the precursor of homicide.

As for second-chance opportunities, most young men who are caught up in a homicide as perpetrator or victim, have had multiple earlier brushes with the law, including periods in reform school, jail, or prison. Although one might be able to point to a few exceptions where incarceration has lead to favorable changes in the individual's value structure, education, and work, for most individuals incarceration is dysfunctional. Faced with a great number of competing demands for scarce resources, our society has seldom been willing to make the order of investment that would provide true second-chance opportunities for those who have faltered.

Marginal Labor Force Role

The diverse sources of ineffective performance in late adolescence and early adulthood outlined above help to explain the last specific category that we will review, namely, the large numbers of young adults, particularly those from low-income minority families, who fail to make an effective linkage to the world of work.

Much of the explanation for their ineffective employment record as adults is embedded in their prior experiences: dropping out of school without ever having acquired the basic competences that employers increasingly demand; failure to have developed a satisfactory work record between the time that they dropped out and their middle-twenties; the additional handicaps that many have acquired by virtue of minor or major run-ins with the criminal justice system, which often prevent their being hired for a range of jobs where a clean record is a prerequisite; experience in the off-the-record economy, including having engaged in illicit or illegal work, which makes them resistant to accepting minimum wage jobs in the regular economy.

Although it would be a mistake to overpromise what new and improved training and employment programs could do to assist in converting potentially marginal workers into regularly attached members of the labor force, it would also be a mistake to give up on a twenty-two or twenty-five-year-old man, especially if he seeks help. Clearly a more effective intervention approach would be one that was instituted earlier so that the adolescent did not drop out of school and was assisted when first entering the labor force.

When it comes to second-chance opportunities, one must recognize that the greater the accumulated deficits of a person, such as functional illiteracy, a poor work history, a criminal record, and the longer the individual has been on the periphery of the labor force and the society, the greater the costs of intervening to help him or her overcome these deficiencies. But before one concludes that the second-chance approach is too costly and its outcome too problematic, it is well to note that forty years of potential marginality is exceedingly costly both to the individual and to society.

The remaining challenge that we face is to identify some of the important findings and implications emerging from the matrix of Figure 2.1, which we have utilized to assess the causes of ineffective behavior among adolescents and young adults and to distinguish between more and less promising types of intervention. In order to keep our conclusions within bounds, we will set out a limited number under each of the following three rubrics: theory, evaluation, and future interventions.

Theory

Shortfalls in the ability of the principal rearing institutions to perform their tasks—the family, the school, and the job market—are the principal sources or causes of ineffective performance among adolescents and young adults. The inability of the family to perform its basic nurturing function either because of the absence of one of the parents and/or deficits in the head of the household foretells trouble because of the difficulties our society has in compensating for such weaknesses. The problem is further compounded by racism, which makes it difficult to develop a cadre of supportive adults who might act as surrogate parents and role models.

Growing up in poorly functioning families and in deteriorating neighborhoods where only an occasional person has a regular job and where only an occasional family lives on income earned from work, many children and adolescents develop early a pessimistic view of themselves and their future as a result of which they see no point in extending themselves to master their school work. Further distortions in their value structure are introduced by their awareness that the only people in their community who have made it, or made it big, are those who are engaged in managing one or another type of illicit activity, a perception that draws many of the young into early crime.

The combination of weak parental guidance and strong corrupting influences in the neighborhood goes far to explain the considerable numbers of young people who early in their adolescence become hooked on drugs, pursue illegal activities, or become pregnant and have a child. Such behavior carries risks but many young people minimize them.

Evaluation of Intervention Efforts

The guiding principle underlying our welfare system, even after its substantial expansion in the 1960s, has been to provide female heads of households and their minor children (and in some states their unemployed husbands) with a level of income in cash and kind that enables them to exist but that has never included additional resources aimed at assisting them to leave the rolls.

On the other hand, appropriations for public education have been handled quite differently. Taxpayers have been willing to increase substantially the amounts of money available to school systems calculated in inflation-free dollars per pupil. A disturbingly large proportion of young people who attend inner-city schools unfortunately continue to terminate their education without having earned a high school diploma and without having acquired the basic competences they need for getting a job and otherwise functioning effectively as adults. Although additional appropriations might be of some help, most analysts believe that the ineffective performance of the ghetto schools is more deeply rooted in inflexible bureaucracies and political power struggles that make significant reforms exceedingly difficult.

Over the last quarter of a century and particularly in the 1962 to 1981 period, the federal government as part of its large initiative with respect to employment and training programs appropriated sizable sums directed to assisting adolescents and young adults. These programs had a great many different objectives, but most experts would agree that only a small minority of enrollees obtained regular jobs.

The wide variety of intervention programs directed at reducing teenage pregnancy have proved to date to be ineffective. A high proportion of the young women who have entered such programs and availed themselves of a broad range of services—counseling, health care, education, child care, job search, and others—have a second out-of-wedlock pregnancy within two years. Unless these teenagers can see a future for themselves that is more attractive than early motherhood, they are likely to continue to give birth to out-of-wedlock offspring.

The institutionalization of young people in medical (psychiatric) centers, drug detoxification units, jails and prisons is often highly dysfunctional as far as their future development is concerned. Individuals with low intelligence as well as limited schooling are a disproportionately large part of the institutionalized population. Because most public facilities operate at or above capacity, they seldom have the resources required to provide any significant amount of rehabilitation. Accordingly, when the confined are released they return to their old haunts and slip back into their former ways.

Directions for Future Initiatives

The thrust of the foregoing analysis has been to call attention to the serious risks that young people face who grow up in families ill equipped to discharge their nurturing responsibilities. If children need nurturing adults and if their immediate family falls short in its ability to provide them with the support they need, substitute mechanisms need to be developed and expanded, which would require active participation by large numbers of dedicated volunteers. This is perhaps the most difficult challenge that our society faces in fashioning more potent intervention programs.

The continuing malfunctioning of most inner-city schools makes it mandatory for any serious reform agenda to deal with this issue. We know how some parents with modest resources have been responding: They enroll their children in a parochial school or relocate the family in a better neighborhood, including the suburbs, where the local public schools perform better. But for many parents neither of the above solutions is feasible. There is considerable support, especially among libertarians and conservatives, for a voucher system, but it is far from clear that its adoption would provide those most in need with a better alternative.

We know that community control of the school system did not provide the answer and that busing has severe limitations especially when children of minority groups represent the majority of those on the school rolls. The following might provide at least some of the leverage that is required to move the large school systems off dead center: How can the success of a few exemplary schools in the inner city be replicated? Would the attraction of a large number of volunteers be feasible and make a difference? Are there practical ways of removing the threat of violence from junior and senior high schools, which makes effective learning exceedingly difficult, if not impossible? What are the prospects that boards of education and the teachers unions might devolve much of their power and responsibility to the principals and teachers of each individual school?

None of these recommendations may prove feasible or, if tried, they might not significantly alter the current poor performance record. But our society must confront this issue and it must keep trying until the results improve, not a little but a lot. It is a quarter century since James Conant put the ghetto school high on the nation's agenda of reform. Progress has been abysmally slow.

In coping with ineffective performance there is something attractive in placing one's bets on preventive efforts rather than ad hoc interventions. But it is no accident that both government and philanthropy have stressed the latter. Great obstacles stand in the way of making the two principal nurturing institutions—the family and the school—perform more effectively for all children, particularly those who live in or close to poverty and belong to minority groups. Blocked by a lack of knowledge, will, and resources to restructure these basic institutions, society understandably has directed its efforts to deal with the dropouts, the misfits, the failures, especially those, like the criminal, whom it sees as a direct threat.

Focusing on the "failures" is also likely to result in the pursuit of a policy of least cost, if one calculates only the social outlays to control deviance and failure and ignores the human losses. The analogy to preventive health is direct and pertinent. Although many expensive screening and treatment programs would pay off in terms of lower morbidity and lessened mortality, overall health expenditures would increase. Accordingly, many preventive efforts are left on the drawing board.

Again, the analogy with the health arena is pertinent. Not all, or even most persons at risk, will, in the absence of screening and treatment, be disabled or die prematurely. The same is true of young people growing up under adverse conditions. Even in the absence of radical social interventions many will surmount their dysfunctional experiences and not become a threat or burden to society. Hence the tendency of society is to focus its efforts on those who fail.

Our society, however, has not been totally unaware and unresponsive to the importance of what we have called process interventions. When family circumstances are viewed by the social welfare staff as being highly dysfunctional for the growth and development of the child, they will place the child out of the home. Unfortunately, the record of children brought up in such alternative environments is not encouraging. Headstart has been another process intervention. Advocates claim a great deal for it while the skeptics are more circumspect. The latter acknowledge that poor children who have been in a Headstart program for a year or two may start off in the first grade more or less on an equal footing with children from middle-class homes, but in the absence of special assistance later on, they contend that the Headstart youngsters will slip back. It is difficult to see why this should not occur.

Over the last several decades in response to the civil rights movement, many private schools, camps, and other educational, cultural and recreational groups have gone out of their way to recruit talented youngsters from minority homes both to make a contribution to their development and also to provide their clientele with an opportunity to interact with a broader cross-section of the population. Although some of the recruited minority youngsters found their new environment difficult and oppressive, most have been able to adjust and to profit from the opportunity. But only a very small number of minority youngsters have been singled out for special attention.

Second-Chance Interventions

The developmental process itself has some built-in aspects of a second chance. Psychologists have long recognized that adolescence often provides the individual with an opportunity to reorder his or her underlying emotional system and motivational structure. And many observers have noted that after the turmoil of adolescence, many young adults again have the opportunity to reorganize how they act and react to forces, internal and external. Moreover, the need to confront new situations such as a job or marriage also leave their mark on many young adults. But having called attention to these built-in potentials for change, individuals must still make use of the building blocks that they have accumulated earlier.

Second-chance interventions have long been incorporated into this and other societies, for example, when men (and now women) have an opportunity to enlist in one of the armed forces—a practice that was long attractive to black men in the South and remains so today. The practice of sending a poorly functioning youngster from a high-income family to a military academy was predicated on the same principle—a radical transfer into an environmental setting with strict discipline could result in positive changes in behavior. A modified second-chance opportunity, introduced in 1964—residential Job Corps centers—has provided a year of intensive remediation for some of the most disadvantaged youth from the ghetto; and for those who stayed the course (about one in three) it provided further transitional assistance to return to school, enter the Armed Forces, or secure an apprenticeship. As noted earlier, institutionalization for serious offenders has seldom proved a constructive experience because of the lack of resources for remedial programs.

There are a variety of short-term, second-chance opportunities that are made available to limited numbers of youngsters from low-income homes, which enable them to spend a month or two during the summer on a farm or some similar setting where they are exposed to radically different conditions than they have previously experienced. Anecdotal reports suggest that some young people respond positively to such changes in scene and in the people with whom they interact.

It needs to be stressed that in a world of constrained resources, the sponsors of second-chance programs, especially those that run for a year or more, must be in a position to cover the board, keep, and transportation costs, which alone amount to $5,000 or more per young person. Sometimes, as in the case of summer farm employment, the labor of the young person can cover part of these costs; the same was true for the work that the Civilian Conservation Corps contributed in beautifying the national parks. But residential costs come high, and this is one reason why the federal government in more recent years has added only nonresidential Job Corps centers.

There are a great many second-chance opportunities available in most urban environments: for high school dropouts the chance to return to school and acquire a GED; for dropouts and high school graduates to take courses in community colleges; for the young person to leave his job and explore another. In earlier days, and to a limited extent even today, going to sea represented such a second chance.

A Few Concluding Observations

Ineffective performance among youth and young adults should not be conceptualized in terms of the medical model of acute-care interventions. If the medical model is to be used, the appropriate one would be the management of chronic diseases where multiple causes are present and where only a few lend themselves readily to modification.

The personality structures of adolescents and young adults have been shaped by their experiences and responses over fifteen to twenty-five years. This should serve as a potent reminder that any external interventions to alter the behavior patterns and/or competences of the individual will not come easily or cheaply.

As adjustment to adulthood requires the individual to be able to hold down a regular job and since only individuals who meet some minimum level of competence will be hired, the direction for many intervention programs is thus prescribed.

It would clearly be preferable to improve the motivation of young people to acquire competences while they are still in the educational process and to improve the capability of the schools to meet this challenge. One way to encourage such behavior on the part of adolescents is to link their performance in school to immediate and longer-term rewards, for instance, by providing part-time jobs to those who pass all their subjects, and by promising them special career help if and when they earn their diplomas.

Because of the critical role that the individual must play in changing himself or herself, most intervention programs should be structured to encourage those who seek self-improvement the opportunity to do so. However, the scarcity of resources requires that such remedial programs be targeted exclusively to those who need the opportunity, not to those who can make it on their own.

Only programs that are substantial in terms of time and resources are likely to prove successful for disadvantaged young people who need intensive assistance to change themselves, their skills, and their goals.

Notes

1. Marc A. Lalonde, *New Perspective on the Health of Canadians* (Ottawa: Information Canada, 1974).

2. Louise B. Russell, *Is Prevention Better than Cure?* (Washington, D.C.: The Brookings Institution, 1986).

3. National Commission for Employment Policy (Eli Ginzberg, chairman), *Tell Me About Your School* (Washington, D.C.: 1979).

3

Drunk Drivers

The leading cause of death among U.S. teenagers is motor vehicle accidents, chiefly among drivers under the influence of alcohol. Nearly half of all deaths of sixteen- to nineteen-year-olds occur as a result of automobile crashes. Although teens in this age group constituted 8 percent of the U.S. population and 9 percent of all licensed drivers in 1977, they accounted for 17 percent of all motor vehicle–related fatalities.[1] Alcohol plays a major role in automobile accidents among all age groups. It is estimated that over 60 percent of all auto fatalities are alcohol related, and alcohol plays an especially important role in fatal crashes involving teenagers. The urgent policy question is whether and through what types of intervention this disturbingly high loss of life can be reduced at a cost that society is willing to accept.

It must be noted at the outset that definitive answers to this challenge are not currently available, among other reasons because there have been relatively few specific interventions aimed at accomplishing this goal; the efforts have not been sustained for sufficient periods of time; and much of the existent data about different types of intervention are at best suggestive, at worst equivocal. Some amplification of this caveat will help to frame the complexities of the issue and the need for caution in reaching definitive judgments about which courses of action should or should not be followed.

To begin with, the automobile is an essential element of daily life in advanced economies for transportation to school, to work, to play, etc. Furthermore, the use of alcohol is an intrinsic feature of the social life of most groups, if not of every individual. Accordingly, it is very difficult for a society to move strongly to deny access to either cars or liquor to any adult group in the population. Pushed to the extreme, denial of the right to drive can deprive a person of the ability to earn a living, which, in turn, could force society to provide public funds for his/her support.

The other critical consideration that helps to conceptualize the challenge is that by definition, the focus is on "teenagers," a discrete if not easily characterized group. Teenagers do not remain teenagers, however, and therefore interventions directed at them must be assessed in terms of delayed effects as they age and enter their twenties. It is not too difficult to conceive a scenario whereby teenage deaths could be significantly reduced, but the death rate among persons in their early twenties would rise disproportionately.

A basic reason for the focus on teenagers, over and above the desire to prevent unnecessary loss of life and injury, is that adolescents are the easiest group to keep from having sanctioned access to alcohol and to keep from sanctioned driving. This is borne out by the following data:

- Of the more than 44,000 auto deaths in 1984, the subtotal for the fifteen to twenty age group came to about 8,100 or 18.2 percent of all fatalities. The twenty-one to twenty-four age group accounted for about 6,300 or 14.2 percent, a proportion not too different from the teenagers (see Table 3.1).
- The percentage of alcohol-related fatalities is considerably higher among the twenty to twenty-four age group (68 percent) than among those fifteen to nineteen (51 percent) (see Table 3.2).
- Between the ages of sixteen and twenty-four, the total number of accidents in each successive year varies from a low of about 150,000 (for sixteen- to seventeen-year olds) to a high of over 200,000 (for twenty-two to twenty-four year olds). The proportion of alcohol-related accidents increases in general with age, from a low of 8.4 percent in the sixteen to seventeen age group to 15.3 percent among the twenty-two to twenty-four age group (see Table 3.3).

These data underscore the need for caution against focusing exclusively on teenagers. Clearly, young people between the ages of twenty-one and twenty-four are also a highly vulnerable group. Yet it would be considerably more difficult to design and implement intervention programs that would have an impact on this older age cohort.

Accordingly, this chapter will (1) provide basic background on concepts and statistics related to drinking and driving; (2) examine the results of various intervention programs focused on adolescent drunk driving; and (3) evaluate the effectiveness of these programs.

TABLE 3.1
Automobile Fatalities by Age, Sex, and Role, 1984

	Under 15	15-17	18-20	Subtotal 15-20	21-24	25-34	35-44	45-54	55-64	65+	Total[a]
Driver	149	1,297	3,225	4,522	4,248	6,609	3,465	2,079	1,850	2,632	25,582
Other occupant	1,433	1,239	1,518	2,757	1,419	1,685	776	577	621	1,342	10,689
Nonoccupant	1,468	331	486	817	625	1,211	787	655	738	1,524	7,970
Total	3,050	2,867	5,229	8,096	6,292	9,505	5,028	3,311	3,209	5,498	44,241
Males	1,879	1,957	3,987	5,944	4,902	7,356	3,635	2,317	2,105	3,208	31,529
Females	1,170	910	1,242	2,156	1,390	2,148	1,393	994	1,104	2,289	12,700

[a]Totals include unknowns.

Source: Fatal Accident Reporting System, 1984 (Washington, D.C.: National Highway Traffic Safety Administration, DOT HS 806–919, February 1986).

TABLE 3.2
Alcohol-Related Automobile Fatalities by Age, 1984

Age	Number of Fatalities	National Estimates of Alcohol-Related Fatalities	Percentage Alcohol-Related[a]
Under 15	3,050	700	23.0%
15–19	6,318	3,250	51.0
20–24	8,070	5,550	68.0
25–64	21,053	12,650	60.0
64+	5,498	1,225	22.0
Total	44,241[b]	23,375	53.0

[a]Based on data from fifteen states with good alcohol-related accident collection.
[b]Total contains unknowns.

Source: Fatal Accident Reporting System, 1984 (Washington, D.C.: National Highway Traffic Safety Administration, DOT HS 806–919, February 1986).

TABLE 3.3
Proportion of Alcohol Involvement in Injury Accidents by Age, National Accident Sampling System (NASS) Data, 1979–1980

Age Group	Number of Injury Accidents	Proportion of Accidents Involving Each Age Group — Drivers with Alcohol	Proportion of Alcohol Involvement in Accidents Occurring During Day 4 AM–8 PM	Night 8 PM–4 AM
16–17	297,000	8.4%	2.8%	20.7%
18	192,000	9.8	4.8	22.9
19	189,000	13.6	3.1	34.0
20	141,000	13.7	6.9	24.0
21	191,000	12.2	5.8	23.6
22–24	407,000	15.3	7.6	37.2
25–44	1,149,000	14.1	7.4	29.4
45–54	327,000	10.1	4.4	28.7
55–64	246,000	8.0	3.7	25.6
65+	178,000	4.6	2.9	20.6
Total	3,317,000			

Source: James C. Fell, *Alcohol Involvement in Traffic Accidents: Recent Estimates from the National Center for Statistics and Analysis* (Washington, D.C.: National Center for Statistics and Analysis, DOT HS 806–269, May 1982).

Background Concepts and Statistics

How Much Drinking Does It Take to Become Intoxicated?

At a blood alcohol content (BAC) of 0.10, almost 50 percent of all people will show overt signs of intoxication. Some people will show such signs at a BAC level of 0.02 or lower. Conversely, others who are frequent drinkers may not appear intoxicated until a BAC of 0.20 is reached. Body weight and metabolism rate also affect the amount of alcohol needed to be consumed to produce signs of intoxication. Thus, a 100-fold difference exists in alcohol tolerance. In most states, the criterion of intoxication is defined as a BAC level of 0.08 or 0.10. This is generally assumed to be equivalent to taking three or four drinks within the period of an hour, although here, too, there are widespread differences, depending on the amount of alcohol in the drink, whether food is consumed, and the characteristics of the individual who is drinking.

What Method Is Used to Determine Whether Alcohol
Is Involved in a Traffic Accident or Fatality?

There are two basic mechanisms used to assess the involvement of alcohol in automotive accidents. In the case of fatalities, BAC levels are the conventional measure. There are only fifteen states, however, with accurate statistical data on BAC in fatal accidents, and most studies of national incidence extrapolate from these fifteen "good" states. There are many occasions when a BAC cannot be taken for procedural reasons, and in cases where over four hours elapse between the fatality and the BAC measurement, the alcohol may have metabolized out of the system. The second method used to measure alcohol involvement is the police report. Almost all accident report forms contain a box to be checked if the investigating police officer has reason to believe that alcohol was involved. Because this determination may later be subject to legal challenge, police tend to be conservative in recording such judgments.

Alcohol involvement in nonfatal accidents is much more problematic, depending on whether the accident is reported and considerations of civil rights, which tend to limit BAC testing. Data on accidents are much less reliable than data on fatalities.

What Is the Extent of Alcohol Involvement in Auto Fatalities?

Based on a large number of studies, approximately 60 percent of drivers involved in fatal accidents have been drinking (i.e., found to have a BAC level above 0.01), and about 45 percent of drivers involved

TABLE 3.4
Proportion of Alcohol Involvement in Fatal Accidents by Age, 1980[a]

Age Group	Number of Fatal Accidents	Proportion of Accidents Involving Each Age Group Drivers with Alcohol	Proportion of Alcohol Involvement in Accidents Occurring During	
			Day 4 AM–8 PM	Night 8 PM–4 AM
16–17	901	36.6%	19.0%	53.6%
18	758	43.9	25.2	59.3
19	788	47.5	23.7	66.1
20	718	47.2	29.5	63.2
21	698	49.6	33.6	63.4
22–24	1,892	50.4	35.2	64.0
25–44	5,434	47.6	30.8	67.7
45–54	1,407	30.4	21.8	46.8
55–64	1,028	26.0	19.7	41.3
65+	860	14.3	11.4	31.0
Total	14,484			

[a]Based on data from fifteen states with complete information.

Source: James C. Fell, *Alcohol Involvement in Traffic Accidents: Recent Estimates from the National Center for Statistics and Analysis* (Washington, D.C.: National Center for Statistics and Analysis, DOT HS 806–269, May 1982).

in fatal accidents were driving while intoxicated (i.e., a BAC level over 0.10). Thus, almost one-half of all automobile fatalities are alcohol related.

Of the 44,000 automobile fatalities in 1984, 43 percent of the fatally injured drivers were legally intoxicated (down from 50 percent in 1980 and 46 percent in 1983). Forty-six percent of the fatally injured drivers in 1984 were sober. Over 50 percent of fatally injured pedestrians in 1984 were intoxicated.

Table 3.4 provides data from the fifteen states that keep reasonably comprehensive statistics on alcohol involvement in motor vehicle fatalities. In 1980, 1,373 (43.3 percent) of 3,165 deaths of adolescents aged sixteen to twenty had alcohol involvement, with well over half of the fatalities occurring between 8 PM and 4 AM.

Teenagers have a high proportion of the alcohol-related fatalities per 100 million vehicle-miles traveled, almost three times the rate of drivers aged twenty-five to forty-four. In absolute numbers, teens accounted for 5,675 of the 25,000 alcohol-related fatalities (22.7 percent) in 1980 (Table 3.5).

TABLE 3.5
Alcohol-Involved Fatal Accident Rates by Driver Age, 1980

Driver Age	Driver License Population[a] (percentage)	Vehicle-Miles Traveled[a] (percentage)	Vehicle-Miles Traveled (100 million miles)	Alcohol-Related Fatal Accidents		Alcohol-Related Accident Rate (100 million vehicle-miles)
				Number	Percentage	
16–17	3.2	1.95	295	1,350	5.4	4.58
18	2.2	1.97	298	1,375	5.5	4.61
19	2.4	2.31	349	1,550	6.2	4.44
20	2.5	2.74	414	1,400	5.6	3.38
Teens Subtotal	10.3	8.97	1,356	5,675	22.7	4.18
21	2.6	2.31	349	1,425	5.7	4.08
22–24	7.0	8.38	1,266	3,925	15.7	3.10
25–44	42.1	46.88	7,081	10,625	42.5	1.50
45–54	12.8	17.53	2,648	1,750	7.0	0.66
55–64	12.4	10.72	1,619	1,100	4.4	0.68
65+	10.6	5.10	770	500	2.0	0.71
Total			15,089	25,000	100.0	1.65

[a]Does not equal 100 percent because drivers under age sixteen are excluded.

Source: Alcohol and Highway Safety 1984: A Review of the State of the Knowledge (Washington, D.C.: National Highway Traffic Safety Administration, DOT HS 806–569, February 1985).

TABLE 3.6
Automobile Fatalities by Road Type and Land Use, 1984

| | | | Total | |
Road Type	Urban	Rural	Number	Percentage
Interstate	2,042	2,256	4,298	9.7
Primary	10,816	10,500	21,316	48.2
Secondary	1,456	6,540	7,996	18.0
Nonfederal aid roads	4,224	6,206	10,430	23.6
Total	18,538	25,502	44,241[a]	

[a]Includes unknowns.

Source: Fatal Accident Reporting System, 1984 (Washington, D.C.: National Highway Traffic Safety Administration, DOT HS 806–919, February 1986).

Who Is Involved in Automobile Accidents and Where Do They Occur?

In general, males have more accidents than females. Although men have 52 percent of the driver's licenses in the United States, they account for 70 percent of the vehicle-miles traveled and for 69 percent of the accidents (1981). Ninety percent of fatally injured drivers are males. Most accidents happen on weekend nights (after midnight), particularly those involving younger drivers aged fifteen to nineteen. Most fatal accidents are single-vehicle crashes and most occur on rural backroads (Tables 3.6 and 3.7).

How Much Alcohol Is Consumed Annually in the United States?

Statistics show everyone over fourteen consumes approximately two alcoholic drinks per day. Because 35 percent of the public claims to abstain totally from alcohol, the number works out closer to three drinks per day. It is known, however, that 11 percent of the adult population consumes 50 percent of all the alcohol sold in the United States. Forty-nine percent of the alcohol sold is beer, 12 percent wine, and 39 percent liquor. Beer is the favorite drink of adolescents, and its consumption tends to be limited primarily by the volume that can be consumed.

What Is the Relationship Between Age and Alcohol-Related Vehicle Fatalities in the United States?

The sixteen to twenty age group represents 10.3 percent of the licensed population. They account for 9 percent of the vehicle-miles traveled and

TABLE 3.7
Automobile Fatalities by Day of Week and Hour of Day, 1984

Day	10 PM– 2 AM	2 AM– 6 AM	6 AM– 10 AM	10 AM– 2 PM	2 PM– 6 PM	6 PM– 10 PM	Total[a]
Sun	1,980	1,422	523	720	1,253	1,536	7,512
Mon	893	477	654	757	1,183	1,157	5,147
Tue	810	439	640	682	1,122	1,040	4,771
Wed	996	420	650	705	1,126	1,155	5,089
Thu	1,189	549	630	730	1,124	1,222	5,491
Fri	1,783	655	698	846	1,413	1,771	7,211
Sat	2,424	1,675	689	884	1,377	1,877	9,009
Total	10,075	5,637	4,484	5,324	8,598	9,758	44,241

[a]Totals include unknowns.

Source: Fatal Accident Reporting System, 1984 (Washington, D.C.: National Highway Traffic Safety Administration, DOT HS 806–919, February 1986).

for 22.7 percent of the alcohol-related fatalities (1980). The next older age cohort, those twenty-one to twenty-four years old, accounts for 21.4 percent of the alcohol-related fatalities but only 9.6 percent of the licensed drivers and 10.6 percent of the vehicle-miles traveled (Table 3.8). Thus, the problem is not simply an adolescent problem, although the teen dimension is easier to control, either through limiting alcohol availability or limiting driving.

What Are the Socioeconomic Variables Associated with Alcohol-Related Driving Accidents?

The socioeconomic variables associated with alcohol-related driving accidents include

- Married drivers have more accidents than nonmarried drivers.
- Lower occupational levels are overrepresented among drinking drivers (although this may be correlated with greater nighttime driving).
- Lower educational levels are correlated with higher BAC levels.
- Alcohol has a more potent effect on less experienced drivers— young teens and women.

In addition, people with a history of previous accidents have higher BAC levels than people without such histories. People with previous

TABLE 3.8
Driver Age and Alcohol Involvement in Accidents, NASS Data, 1979–1980 (in percentages)

Driver Age	Driver License Population	Vehicle Miles Traveled	All Accident Drivers	Age Group with Alcohol Involvement	All Alcohol-Involved Accident Drivers
16–17	3.2	1.95	7.9	4.0	4.8
18	2.2	1.97	4.8	6.7	4.9
19	2.4	2.31	4.6	7.9	5.5
20	2.5	2.74	3.9	8.7	5.1
21	2.6	2.31	4.2	9.1	5.8
22–24	7.0	8.38	10.0	10.6	16.3
25–34	25.0	27.40	23.5	6.6	24.0
35–44	17.1	19.48	12.6	5.9	11.4
45–54	12.8	17.53	9.7	8.9	13.2
55–64	12.4	10.72	6.5	4.8	4.8
65+	10.6	5.10	5.5	2.8	2.4

Source: James C. Fell, *Alcohol Involvement in Traffic Accidents: Recent Estimates from the National Center for Statistics and Analysis* (Washington, D.C.: National Center for Statistics and Analysis, DOT HS 806–269, May 1982).

enforcement actions against them have higher BAC levels. This may indicate a group of heavy drinkers for whom punitive actions have been ineffective.

What Are the Different Theories
About the Effects of Drinking on Driving?

In general, four theories have been advanced to explain the effects of drinking on driving. These are discussed in turn below.

Skill theories. Driving takes a certain amount of skill, which is adversely affected by higher BAC levels. With greater driving experience, there are fewer accidents. Illustrative of the evidence supporting this theory is the fact that most motorcycle accidents happen during the first six months of ownership. On the other hand, lack of experience in driving and young age tend to go together, so it is not clear what is lacking—skill, maturity, or some combination of both.

Spare capacity. This theory postulates that drivers have a limited capacity to deal with complex situations and that alcohol "uses up" that spare capacity. However, most drunk driving accidents do not occur in situations that are particularly complex (e.g., intersections) but rather on lightly traveled country roads.

FIGURE 3.1
Teenage Drinkers and Drivers as a Subset of Drinkers and Drivers

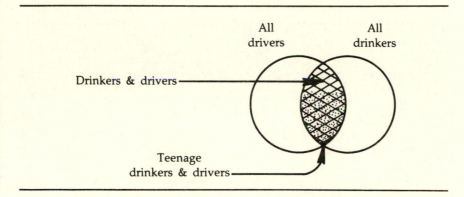

Risk-taking theories. These theories maintain that drivers operate with interdependent probability systems, one for objective risk assessment and one for subjective risk assessment. Drinking, it is argued, confuses these two sets of probabilities and leads to greater risk-taking.

Risk-compensation theories. These theories postulate that drivers operate at a fixed level of subjective risk-taking. Factors that increase the perception of driving as being safer—seat belts, better roads, good weather—lead the driver to take more risks—drive faster, drink and drive. Those factors that tend to increase the perception of driving as unsafe encourage the driver to take fewer risks. The implication of this theory is that as external factors are improved, people will take greater risks. It has been noted that the perception that a road is safe leads people to feel confident about speeding; at the same time people tend to slow down if road conditions are not good. It has been found that drunk drivers tend to use their seat belts less frequently than sober drivers, and also tend to be driving faster than the speed limit at the time of their accident. This may indicate that the drinking interferes with their subjective perceptions of reality.

Programs Aimed at
Reducing Teenage Drunk Driving

Drunk driving accidents are a small subset of two independent but complementary activities—drinking and driving. Teenage drunk driving is an even smaller subset of the above activity, best expressed through set theory shown in Figure 3.1. Given the relationship depicted in the figure, it is obvious that it is easier to develop interventions that affect the larger sets (all drivers and all drinkers) than to develop programs aimed specifically at adolescents. There are, however, two important factors that belie this observation: (1) people are first licensed to drive during teenage years and (2) people are first allowed to buy alcoholic beverages during teenage years. Thus, in this particular case, it is possible to directly target adolescents with specific intervention programs.

Certain facts about teenagers and drunk driving are important in this regard:

- Teenagers drink and drive less often than older drivers. When they do drink and drive, teens tend to have lower blood alcohol content levels.
- In both fatal and nonfatal crashes, teens are less likely than older drivers to have been drinking.
- Teenage drivers who drink are more likely than older drivers to be involved in crashes. Compared with older drivers, teens with low and moderate blood alcohol content levels are much more likely to incur crashes.

Thus, although fewer teenagers than adults drink and drive, the risk of crashing for teens is considerably higher when they do drink. This has been attributed to the relative inexperience of teens with drinking and with driving after drinking.

The major factors that are involved with adolescent automobile accidents are thus access to alcohol, access to driving, and inexperience with driving. From an epidemiological perspective, it follows that interventions should center around limiting the exposure of teens to alcohol, keeping teens from driving, and increasing teenagers' experience with driving.

Preventive Intervention and Strategies

Intervention programs aimed at reducing adolescent automobile accidents can be classified by their approach to the problems. Preventive efforts are those that seek to keep teenagers from driving or keep teenagers from drinking. In this usage, these are primary prevention activities. Deterrent activities seek to keep teens who have been drinking from driving. In this usage, deterrent activities are a variant of secondary prevention. We also examine technological, community, and long-term programs.

Controlling Access to Alcohol

One of the major strategies aimed at reducing adolescent alcohol-related auto accidents and fatalities is limiting the access of teenagers to alcohol. In general, this has been done by raising the legal drinking age, but it can also be accomplished by raising the price of alcoholic beverages and/or decreasing their alcohol content. There is little question that if the ability to obtain alcohol is constrained, alcohol-related accidents will also be constrained. What is questionable, however, is how effective such constraining efforts will be and what are the sequelae of restricting access to alcohol.

Raising the drinking age. After the failure of nationwide prohibition, states were left free to set their legal drinking ages. Most states set the minimum drinking age at twenty-one. By the early 1970s, after eighteen-year-olds had secured the right to vote, it seemed incongruous that a teen could vote and be drafted into the armed forces, but could not legally drink. As a result, many states lowered their legal drinking age to eighteen. Reports soon indicated that the number of automobile fatalities among teens that were alcohol-related increased rapidly. Since the mid-1970s, no state has lowered its legal drinking age and many states have restored their earlier lower limit of twenty-one. In July 1984, President Ronald Reagan signed legislation that required states to adopt a minimum drinking age of twenty-one by 1987 or face a 5 percent reduction in their federal highway funds and a 10 precent reduction if they failed to act by 1988. In signing the legislation, President Reagan said: "With the problem so clear-cut and the proven solution at hand, we have no misgivings about this judicious use of federal power."[2] As of mid-1986, there are nine states with legal drinking ages of less than twenty-one (Colorado, Idaho, Louisiana, Montana, Ohio, South Dakota, Wisconsin, Wyoming, and the District of Columbia). Another sixteen states have a minimum drinking age of twenty-one, but for technical reasons have not been certified by the Department of Transportation as complying with all the requirements of the new federal legislation.

Numerous studies have examined the effectiveness of raising the drinking age to reduce auto fatalities. The vast majority indicate some degree of effectiveness in the short term and a subsequent reversal after the initial few years. There have been no good studies of the long-term effectiveness of this strategy. It must be noted that there are serious methodological problems with most studies due to the use of proxy measures, inadequate data collection, and failure to use a long-term time frame or to account for alternative explanations of the results. Five of these studies are reviewed below.

1. One study focused on the effects legislation had on raising the drinking age in Michigan from eighteen to twenty-one in December

1978. The study examined data from 1972 to 1979 and, through the use of modeling techniques, found a 31 percent reduction in expected alcohol-related crashes for drivers eighteen to twenty in 1979. Alcohol-related crashes for drivers twenty-one to twenty-four were 9 percent above expected values, and alcohol-related crashes for drivers twenty-five to forty-five were 5 percent higher than expected.[3]

2. Another study examined the effects of raising the minimum drinking age in Maine (from eighteen to twenty) in October 1977. The author found some decline in accidents among eighteen-year-olds and little or no decline among nineteen-year-olds.[4]

3. Another study was conducted on the impact of increasing the legal drinking age in Illinois. This study found that one year after the drinking age was raised from eighteen to twenty in January 1980, there was a decrease of 8.8 percent in male single-vehicle nighttime accidents.[5]

4. One study examined the effect of raising the minimum drinking age on involvement in fatal crashes. This report analyzed data from nine states (Illinois, Iowa, Maine, Massachusetts, Michigan, Minnesota, Montana, New Hampshire, Tennessee) that raised their drinking age between 1977 and 1980 and compared those states with others that did not raise their drinking age. The study concluded that any state that raises its legal drinking age can expect a 28 percent decline in fatal nighttime crashes.[6]

5. Another study focused on alcohol-related traffic deaths in fifteen states that raised their drinking age between 1979 and 1983. It was found that in thirteen of the fifteen states, there was no significant change in the percentage of alcohol-related fatalities in the affected age group.[7] The authors of this study explain their "perverse" conclusions as the result of an alternative methodology based on the use of the percentage of fatalities rather than the actual number of fatalities. In addition, the authors point out that because the overall automobile fatality rate has been falling, alcohol-related fatalities can increase proportionately while falling in absolute terms. The authors conclude that raising the drinking age is not an effective means of reducing adolescent automobile fatalities.

Clearly, limiting the exposure of teens to alcohol should limit their ability to drink and drive. The question is, however: Is raising the legal drinking age an effective method? Adolescents who really want to drink do not find it difficult to obtain alcoholic beverages through their home, through complacent liquor store or bar owners, or through other means. If there is nationwide adoption of a federal minimum legal drinking age of twenty-one, then the problem of jumping state boundaries to areas with lower drinking ages will be eliminated. Nevertheless, a legal drinking age is not the same as eliminating access to alcohol. Yet, it is a politically easy way for legislators to show that they are concerned with the problem of adolescent drunk driving and has therefore become the preferred method for seeking a reduction in drunk-driving accidents.

Raising the price of alcohol. An alternative method of limiting access to alcoholic beverages involves raising the price. Economists have found a high price elasticity for alcohol consumption: Raising prices will lower the amount consumed. Douglas Coate and Michael Grossman argue that an increase in the federal excise tax on beer (the alcoholic beverage most used by teenagers) will result in a decrease in beer consumption among youths, particularly among those who drink frequently (four to seven times per week).[8] The authors note that the real price of liquor has actually fallen substantially between 1960 and the present, and a major reason for this has been the federal excise tax on alcoholic beverages that has been in effect since 1951. Because adolescents prefer beer to other alcoholic beverages, raising the excise tax on beer would have a significant impact on its consumption. The authors argue that such a tax increase in conjunction with an age twenty-one minimum drinking law would substantially reduce alcohol-related fatalities among adolescents.

Of course, teenagers are not the sole or principal consumers of beer, and it would be politically difficult, if not impossible, to gain passage of a law that would significantly increase the cost of drinking beer for all persons, even though the law would be focused on altering the behavior of a small subgroup of the population.

Decreasing the alcohol content of beverages. It has been noted that adolescents prefer beer to other kinds of alcoholic beverages. As there is a physiological limit on the quantity of beer that can be consumed at one sitting, one potential mechanism of reducing the blood alcohol content (BAC) of drinking teens would be to lower the alcohol content of beer. Although this would be difficult to implement, the effects could be significant, because without changing consumption patterns, BAC levels could be lowered. Benefits from such a measure would extend to the entire beer-drinking population, but its greatest effects would be on adolescents.

Although low-alcohol and even no-alcohol beers have recently been introduced, they have not been marketed with the sophistication and glitter that conventional alcoholic beverages receive. Given this low-level marketing thrust, it is unlikely that such beverages will have much of an impact on drinking habits.

Restricting Access to Driving

A second set of preventive approaches to reduce adolescent auto accidents is based on restricting access to driving. The less time spent in a car, the lower the accident rate. In general, these approaches fall into four categories: (1) raising the age of licensure; (2) curfews on nighttime driving; (3) eliminating high school driver education courses; and (4) probationary licensure.

Raising the age of licensure. All states permit licensure at age fifteen or sixteen, with the exception of New Jersey, which has a minimum age of seventeen. Even though without alcohol involvement the accident and fatality rate for adolescents is substantial, raising the age of licensure should have a significant impact on teen automobile fatality and injury rates. It is presumed that this will result from less exposure to driving and to greater maturity when the individual is finally licensed. The results from New Jersey have been especially promising: Between 1975 and 1980, there were only four deaths among sixteen-year-old drivers, compared with eighteen in Massachusetts and twenty-six in Connecticut.[9]

Most states make allowances for the need to drive at younger ages in the case of families involved in certain occupations, such as agriculture. Nevertheless, a primary method for reducing teenage driving accidents would be to limit the ability of teens to drive. Yet delaying the age of licensure may prove to be an excessive economic burden for teens, who may not be able to work without access to an automobile, as well as a social burden to families, which must continue to transport adolescents to social activities.

Nighttime curfews. Although only 20 percent of the total mileage of teen drivers is accumulated between 9 PM and 6 AM, over 50 percent of fatalities occur during those hours. The highest death rate for all drivers is for sixteen-year-old males at night.[10] Another strategy for reducing accidents is to limit the ability of teens to drive at night through the use of curfews. The licensing systems of most states have a learner's permit category, which allows a person in the process of obtaining a driver's license to drive if a licensed adult is present in the car (i.e., the learner cannot drive alone). In most cases, learner's permits enable the learner to drive earlier (generally six months) than the legal age of licensure.

Curfew laws take this process a step further by restricting the ability of a teenage license-holder to drive at particular times—in essence by providing a limited license. New York State (excluding New York City and Long Island) allows drivers to obtain a license at sixteen, but prohibits sixteen- and seventeen-year-olds who have not taken driver education from driving between 9 PM and 5 AM. The curfew is waived for sixteen- and seventeen-year-olds accompanied by a parent or driving to and from work or school. Louisiana, which licenses at age fifteen, restricts fifteen- and sixteen-year-olds from driving between 11 PM and

5 AM, and has no exemptions or waivers. Studies have found lower crash involvement in states with curfews.

Nighttime curfew restrictions raise two issues that have not been adequately addressed in the literature—driving experience and illegal driving. Along with access to alcohol and access to driving, a third major factor in predicting auto accidents is exposure to driving. People with more experience have fewer accidents. One reason for this might be that the more one drives, the better one is able to assess risks and take proper defensive actions. If young drivers are prevented from driving at night, it is possible that their lack of experience with such driving will be reflected in a higher frequency of nighttime accidents at the age at which they first become eligible to drive at night. If driving experience is the most critical factor in explaining teenage auto accidents, as some authors have suggested, then nighttime curfews may turn out to have serious limitations when longitudinal studies of their effects become available.

Although it is possible to legislate a curfew on driving at night and to legislate the necessity for a license in order to drive, it is much more difficult to enforce such regulations. The following statistics from data gathered between 1975 and 1978 on all motor vehicle fatalities in the United States bear on this issue: 8.5 percent of drivers under eighteen did not have a valid license for the vehicle they were driving (compared with 3.9 percent of drivers eighteen to twenty and 2.6 percent of drivers over twenty); 48 percent of motorcycle drivers under eighteen did not have a motorcycle license; and 38 percent of motorcycle drivers under eighteen did not have a driver's license either.[11] It is difficult to spot a sixteen- or seventeen-year-old who is driving without a proper license or driving at night without stopping all drivers, a costly enforcement action. As more states seek to limit teenagers from driving, it is likely that the numbers of teens who drive illegally will increase unless enforcement efforts substantially improve.

Eliminating driver-education programs. In almost all states, passing a high school driver's education course entitles the student to obtain a full driver's license between six months to a year earlier than those who do not take such a course. It has long been felt that teaching teens to drive in a school setting where driving safety information and training are included in the course would make teens better drivers. Many auto insurance companies had given explicit support to this approach by offering graduates of such programs reduced auto insurance rates. Recent studies, however, show that because driver education programs allow teens to drive at earlier ages, their ultimate effect is to increase the number of accidents and fatalities among teens. In Connecticut, when several school districts eliminated driver's education programs as a result of a state cutback in funding, not only did teen fatality rates decline, but teens deferred the age at which they obtained a license.

Probationary licenses. Probationary licenses are a variant of the learner's permit. Essentially, if a teen with a learner's permit commits a moving violation, then the teen is ineligible for full licensure for some period (generally six months to a year). The advantage of such a system is that it builds on the desire of teens to obtain a driver's license. The disadvantage is that it requires strict enforcement. Surveys of high school students who self-report their behavior show a far greater incidence of unsafe activity (e.g., speeding, driving after drinking, etc.) than their actual conviction rates indicate. Moreover, only 10 percent of drivers under eighteen who were involved in fatal crashes between 1975 and 1978 had been involved in other reported crashes before the fatal accident, as compared with 25 percent for drivers over eighteen years of age. Only 18 percent of drivers under eighteen who were involved in fatal crashes had convictions for moving violations before their fatal crash, as opposed to 48 percent for drivers over eighteen.[12] Thus, safe driving for a limited time period is not necessarily a good indicator of future accidents. However, by making a full license dependent on a period of safe driving behavior, the probationary license may have a positive influence on future driving practices. It is possible, for example, that such programs may increase the number of teens who use seat belts and thus improve their survival chances in an automobile crash.

Keeping teens from driving will undoubtedly contribute to a lowered automobile fatality rate. However, it is currently unclear what the effects will be on older cohorts who will have less experience in driving. Conceivably, the lack of driving experience will be balanced out by greater maturity and, subsequently, less risk-taking, although the driving statistics for drivers between eighteen to twenty-five do not lend much support to the maturation theory.

The ability to limit driving applies only indirectly to the problem of adolescent drunk driving. However, limitations on driving should reduce the numbers of fatalities and accidents for all teen drivers. A major uncertainty with such programs is their potential acceptance by adolescents and their parents. Not only do adolescents want to drive as early as possible, but also the burden of their parents is eased by teens using the car to perform chores, to transport siblings, and to relieve parents of the responsibility for transporting them. Programs limiting the ability of teens to drive could evoke strong resistance from the public.

However, surveys of adolescents and their parents in states with such programs show an understanding and approval of their aims. Whether this self-reported support on surveys translates into behavioral changes must still be assessed.

Deterrent Interventions and Strategies

The first controls on drinking and driving were mandated in Norway in 1936 and in Sweden in 1941. These laws are considered the classic approaches to deterring drunk driving and drunk drivers. The laws criminalized the act of driving with a BAC above a certain level and established random police roadblocks to test drivers. Drivers with BACs above the legal limit were subject to steep penalties—usually jail for the heavily intoxicated—and fines and license revocation for those less heavily intoxicated. These laws have served as the model for other countries that have attempted to deter drunk driving. The finding that "there is no scientifically valid evidence to date of the deterrent effectiveness of these laws in their home countries" is therefore noteworthy.[13]

After examining the laws and statistical evidence on limiting drinking and driving through deterrence, the author, H. Lawrence Ross, was not sanguine about the results. He concludes that what is needed to make a deterrent system work is constant police enforcement, constant attention by the media, and the subjective belief that a violator will be caught and punished. The critical job is convincing people that if they drive after drinking, they will either have an accident or be caught by the police and prosecuted. Even if the subjective belief can be sustained, it may only deter those who are fearful of the criminal system and the embarrassment of arrest and conviction.

Ross presents impressive data to make his case. He cites a 1978 report by Ralph Jones and Kent Joscelyn for the National Highway Traffic Safety Agency (NHTSA) in which the authors state: "Research suggests that a driver in the United States would have to commit some 200–2,000 DWI (driving while intoxicated) violations to be caught. After apprehension, he would still stand only a 50-50 chance of suffering more than a relatively mild punishment. Such a threat is apparently acceptable even to most social drinkers who are able to control their drinking."[14]

In other work done for the NHTSA, Summers and Harris calculated the conditional probabilities of accident and arrest while driving (depicted in Figure 3.2).[15] What is remarkable about this example is the very low probability of having an accident and the conditional probabilities of arrest. Because the probability of being stopped while DWI on any given trip is well under 1:1,000, it would require more than a twentyfold increase in the probability of arrest to increase the chances of impediment to the trip to 1:100. Even though these probabilities are based on ten-

FIGURE 3.2
Conditional Probabilities of Accident and Arrest While Driving

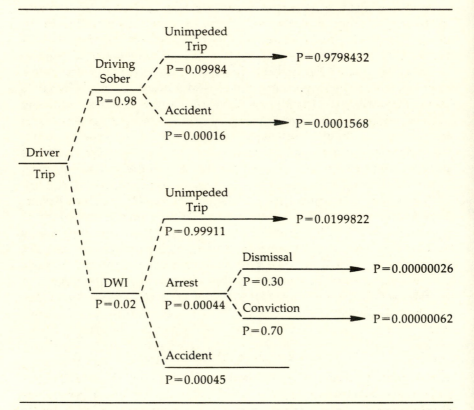

Source: H. Lawrence Ross, *Deterrence of the Drinking Driver: An International Survey* (Washington, D.C.: National Highway Traffic Safety Administration, DOT HS 805—820, March 1981).

year-old data, it is unlikely that police surveillance has improved sufficiently to make more than marginal changes in these rates.

It appears that deterrent programs have a short-term effectiveness that can fade dramatically within a period of a few months to a few years, depending on the level of police involvement. Laws that allow for little discretion in punishment/penalty—that is, those that increase the certainty of punishment and the severity of punishment—can reduce the amount of drinking and driving to the extent that the population at large can be convinced that they will be caught. Although there are few useful long-term studies, most report a diminution in the effectiveness of this approach over time.

Attempts to impose stricter penalties without increasing the certainty of punishment produce no effect on drinking and driving. In some cases, increasing the penalty results, paradoxically, in changes that actually lessen the certainty of application of the penalty, thus resulting in no change in behavior. In these situations, police may underreport violations or shift DWI violations to less severely punishable categories of offense.

One of the major problems with deterrent-based systems is that police have trouble identifying drunk drivers either visually or through behavioral observations. Mandatory roadblocks and BAC testing are constrained by serious questions of constitutional and civil rights as well as by costs.

Most accidents happen when there are few police on patrol (i.e., late at night). Police who are available for the late shift have other crime-control functions and missions to perform. Police departments that try to shift resources to drunk driver detection find that they cannot sustain it for a long enough period of time to exert more than a temporary, if any, deterrent effect. The most effective sites for BAC screening would be near bars and liquor stores, but this has generally led to lawsuits and claims of harassment. Setting up roadblocks on a random basis is not cost-effective, given the resources required to keep them going and the low rate of detection. And even though such random site blockades may have a general deterrent effect, it is usually easy to evade them.

Technological Interventions

The limited success of preventive approaches and the marginal effectiveness of deterrence are viewed as embedded in human nature. As differences in individual perceptions of risk, risk aversion, maturity, self-destructive behavior, and luck militate against the efficacy of such attempts to control drinking and driving, many policymakers have sought the answer in passive technologies that work independently of human factors.

In the same way that automobile safety advocates see the air bag as the future of restraint systems because no way has been found to raise long-term seat-belt compliance rates above 20 percent, those concerned with the dangers of drinking and driving also look to passive systems that will prevent drunk drivers from starting their cars or, if they get on the road, will signal their condition, so that other drivers can take defensive actions.

One such technology, with prototype devices already in production, is an auto ignition system that requires a test of blood alcohol level to be activated. The driver must breathe into a device, and only if the BAC registers below a certain level will the ignition start. Such technology seems to be based more on frustration than promise. These devices may have utility for drivers with several DWI convictions or those on parole, but they would have limited utility for the vast majority of the population. The potential problems with such systems are numerous: They can be removed; they can be fooled (someone will surely market "sober air"); they might fail (i.e., the car would not start even if the driver were sober or would start if he were drunk); they would be expensive; and they would evoke objections from people who habitually do not drive when they drink.

There are several other technological approaches to controlling the drunk driving problem, most of which are aimed at the heavy drinker, rather than the social or occasional drinker. Among these are the following:

1. Having separate brake- and turn-indicators on cars (now a standard feature on newer models). In tests, drivers with a higher BAC were found to drive more safely when the cars in front of them were so equipped.

2. Putting speed governors in automobiles to limit the maximum speed at which the vehicle can travel. Because many alcohol-related auto accidents occur at high speeds, both the number of accidents and their severity might be reduced by such mechanisms.

3. Improving roadway curve delineation. Better signs that warn of approaching curves and the sharpness of such curves might lower the frequency of accidents, particularly on secondary roads.

4. Installing passive erratic performance indicators. These are systems that would automatically detect erratic actions by the driver (such as frequent lateral movement or changes in speed) and flash a warning light, sound a buzzer internally, automatically lower the speed of the vehicle, or flash a signal to oncoming or following cars that care should be taken in approaching the vehicle.

5. Installing drunk driver warning systems so that a driver must pass a skill test before the ignition will start or that flashes a warning to approaching cars if the driver fails to pass the test.

Given the resistance to automobile safety devices exhibited by the U.S. public, it is unlikely that any of these technological approaches will have much impact in the near future.

Community Efforts

Because legislative changes are difficult to enact, many concerned civic groups have sought to fashion voluntary strategies aimed at controlling the adolescent drunk driving problem.

One group that has received particular prominence is Mothers Against Drunk Driving (MADD). Although not focusing exclusively on adolescents, this group has attempted to make the drunk driving problem more visible through frequent appeals to the media and through the continuous, aggressive lobbying of public officials. The organization was founded by the mother of a teen who was killed by a drunk driver, and it has since become a nationwide effort with local chapters in most states. The group frequently protests that sentencing decisions for drunk drivers are too lenient, and MADD has been a potent force in getting state legislatures to raise the legal drinking age.

Another group that has received national attention is Students Against Drunk Driving (SADD). SADD chapters are located primarily in high schools across the country and occasionally in colleges. SADD groups do extensive educational work primarily with student groups. SADD is best known for promoting a contract between an adolescent and his/her parents in which the parent agrees to drive the adolescent home if the adolescent is unfit to drive without asking any questions or punishing the adolescent. In some cases, community projects have been designed with parents "on call" to pick up anyone needing to be driven home who calls during the course of an evening. There have been no scientific studies of the effectiveness of this arrangement, but it seems likely to be of limited utility as it requires the adolescent to make the decision to call home or somewhere else at a time when she/he is already drunk.

Another potentially more effective strategy proposed by SADD and MADD groups is the nondrinking companion—a peer group member who refrains from drinking so as to be able to drive other members of the group home. Strategies of this type have been successful (on an anecdotal basis) in other countries, and they provide an opportunity for nondrinking teens to remain part of the social group.

SADD and MADD work to keep the issue of drunk driving before the public through frequent use of the media and dramatic presentations of the consequences of drunk driving. Media campaigns based on fear tactics have a low rate of effectiveness, once the initial reaction has worn off. This is particularly true for adolescents who have difficulty imagining that what is depicted on television could be real. Because the data show that most adolescent alcohol-involved crashes happen at low BACs, it is not unreasonable that most adolescents cannot imagine themselves getting drunk enough to cause an accident. The impact of warning messages is therefore diluted. The same argument applies to the myriad public service announcements and advertisements that warn against the dangers of drinking and driving. Unless these efforts are reinforced by actual deterrent actions (more police, more random testing, stiffer penalties), and unless these efforts actually succeed in convincing the public that drinking and driving is truly risky, they will have only limited effectiveness.

A review of the material that has been used to combat drinking and driving, including adolescent drinking and driving, reveals seven basic themes:

1. Emphasis (sometimes exaggerated) on the degree of enforcement (e.g., "you will be caught").
2. Fear and unpleasantness of arrest (treatment like a common criminal).
3. Effectiveness of breathanalyzer tests.
4. Citizen-reporting of observed drunk drivers.
5. Special holiday DWI blitzes by police.
6. Humiliation, embarrassment, penalties, or arrest.
7. Premature death or disability.

Secular Improvements

An unequivocal long-term secular decline in U.S. auto fatalities (in terms of fatality rates per 100 million vehicle-miles driven) can be observed, starting in 1940 and continuing to the present. Numerous intervening variables confuse the data interpretation, and care must be taken to distinguish between cross-sectional analysis and time series. The several oil crises and resultant shortages of gasoline; the rising price of gasoline; economic recessions; the lowering of the speed limit to 55 miles per hour; improvements in road safety; and improvements in vehicle safety, all have exerted some impact upon the automobile fatality rate. It can be argued that the increase in drunk driving accidents is a function of the decrease in other sources of accidents; this is different from concluding that there has been an upward trend in drinking and driving. Such an analysis would view the alcohol-involved fatality rate more as a residual problem than a new or exacerbating one.

In 1941, the motor vehicle traffic fatality rate was 11.43 deaths per 100 million vehicle-miles traveled. In 1984, after a steady decline, it was only 2.58 fatalities per 100 million vehicle-miles traveled. Even though in 1984 over 44,000 people died in auto accidents, as opposed to 38,000 in 1941, driving has become a much safer activity. Among the reasons for the improvement in the fatality rate are the following:

- Increased use of seat belts.
- Safer highways: better signs, curve-free roads, the interstate system, safety barriers, rest areas, upgrading of secondary roads, etc.
- Safer cars: better brakes, emergency flashers, improved crash resistance.

- Higher gas prices: less recreational driving, fewer people on the road.
- Economic recessions: fewer people driving to work or driving in relation to their job.
- Lower speed limit, even with suboptimal compliance.
- Improved enforcement efforts: speed traps, radar, etc.

Yet even with these overall improvements, auto accidents and alcohol-related accidents remain the leading cause of death for adolescents. What has made the teenage driving problem of particular concern is that the number of teens who die in car accidents as passengers is almost as large as those who are drivers. Adolescents tend to travel in packs, and many older adolescents transport siblings and friends who are younger than themselves. Teenage drivers also are involved in a greater proportion of "at fault" accidents than older drivers. Furthermore, the deaths for which teen drivers are responsible tend to be concentrated disproportionately among people other than themselves—passengers in their cars, drivers and passengers in other cars, and pedestrians.[16]

Also complicating the problem is the fact that teenage drinking is largely episodic and for the most part social, and it is not possible to identify any group of adolescents who are potential drinking drivers.

The confluence of young age and its attendant lack of maturity, inexperience with drinking and with driving, and the ease of availability of both alcohol and automobiles, are further problems.

Both the automobile and drinking are so embedded in U.S. social and economic life that our society will not tolerate extreme measures to deal with problems created by either. This inescapable fact greatly restricts the methods available and the potential interventions that can be utilized to combat drunk driving.

Statistics point to the operational complexities in grappling with the issues. Alcohol-involved drivers take fewer safety precautions, and this is especially true of teens. Only 2.2 percent of alcohol-involved drivers wore seat belts at the time of their fatal accidents, compared with 7.2 percent of sober drivers. In addition, pedestrians, motorcyclists, and truck drivers account for almost one-third of all automobile fatalities. It has also been shown that drivers who drink heavily have a cavalier attitude toward the law. Suspensions or revocations of licenses and other penalties are often ignored. Therefore, although the percentage of alcohol-related fatalities is decreasing, these types of accidents remain a serious problem.

Evaluating Adolescent Drunk Driving
Reduction Interventions

In attempting to evaluate programs designed to reduce teenage drunk-driving accidents, several factors must be considered:

1. What are the expectations of any specific intervention? Given that it is not possible to entirely eliminate drunk driving, how much reduction in deaths and accidents can be expected?

2. Over how long a time period should interventions be carried out, and for what period of time should evaluations take place? Most studies of drunk driving interventions have not used an evaluation period of more than a year or two after the start of the intervention, and those that have looked at longer time periods uniformly report decreased effectiveness of the program.

3. What are the costs of a particular intervention? Beyond the direct economic costs associated with administering and enforcing a particular program, are the indirect economic costs (lost tax revenues from reduced liquor sales when drinking ages are raised); opportunity costs (increases in residential crime when police are assigned to DWI enforcement); and social costs (potential for turning to other, less controllable, methods of amusement if alcohol is restricted).

4. What are the unintended consequences of a particular intervention? That is, will increased restrictions on driving result in a general disregard for the law and heightened cynicism about social values on the part of adolescents?

5. Will a particular intervention program have an impact that extends beyond the target population? Will, for example, media programs aimed at teenagers also sensitize adults to drunk driving issues?

6. Given the large number of intervening factors, is it possible to evaluate the impact of any one particular intervention with any accuracy?

These factors must all be accounted for in any rigorous evaluation, and from this perspective, there really have been no adequate evaluations of drunk driving programs.

Table 3.9 compares the strategies and interventions discussed in the previous section in terms of their costs and effectiveness, insofar as it is possible to make judgments on these matters. Along with this comparison are comments pertaining to each of the approaches. The parameters for evaluation are as follows:

1. How easy is it to implement this intervention, given the assumption of an active state/local government and a concerned citizenry?

2. How easy is it to enforce the particular intervention, once it is enacted?

3. What are the costs of the intervention to the target group (i.e., teens) in economic and social terms?
4. What are the costs of the intervention to society as a whole in economic and social terms?
5. What is the potential effectiveness of the intervention in reducing adolescent drunk driving accidents?

The interpretation of Table 3.9 does not give much reason to believe that the adolescent drunk driving problem will be soon behind us. In essence, measures that are easy to implement and enforce have the least effectiveness in reducing accidents and fatalities. Measures that have a greater degree of effectiveness come at a much higher cost to society and/or to teenagers.

Although no extant programs can be said to be truly effective in reducing drunk-driving fatalities and accidents, some conclusions about more or less effective programs can be drawn.

- Programs that limit exposure to alcohol and limit the amount of driving are more effective than programs that ignore these targets.
- Programs that offer a reward after a period of exemplary behavior are more effective than programs based on punishment.
- Deterrent programs are only effective when the public believes they will be enforced rigorously.
- Educational programs based on scare tactics have only a limited effect.

The advantages of comprehensive multifaceted adolescent drunk-driving programs have not been explored but seem to hold promise. Raising the legal drinking age, imposing nighttime curfews, using probationary licenses, applying peer-pressure tactics, and widescale education and public information, together with aggressive deterrence through enforcement should prove more effective than any one of these elements applied singly. Moreover, it is possible that experience with more comprehensive multifaceted programs will suggest new approaches to deal with this problem.

Concluding Observations

Drunk driving by adolescents and adults is just one of a great many areas of life where significant numbers of individuals fail to act "rationally" and do not hesistate to break the law. Sexual promiscuity, drugs, crime, and other types of aberrant behavior are also characterized by impulsive behavior, excessive risk-taking, and so forth.

TABLE 3.9
Comparison of Intervention Strategies

Strategy	Ability to Implement	Ability to Enforce	Cost to Teens	
			Economic	Social
1. Raise drinking age	moderate-easy	moderate	low	high
2. Increase tax on beer	difficult	easy	high	low
3. Promote low-alcohol beer	easy	difficult	low	low
4. Raise licensing age	moderate-easy	moderate	moderate	high
5. Nighttime curfew	easy	difficult	low	high
6. Eliminate driver's education	easy	easy	moderate	high
7. Probationary license	easy	moderate	low	low
8. More police patrols	moderate	difficult	low	low
9. Stiffer penalties	easy	moderate	low	low
10. Technological approaches	difficult	difficult	low	low
11. Adolescent-parent contracts	easy	easy	low	low
12. Media and education	easy	easy	low	low

Cost to Society		Potential Effectiveness in Reducing Adolescent Drunk Driving	Comments
Economic	Social		
low	low	moderate-high	1. Teens who want to drink will find a way
high	low	low	1. May lead to switch in consumption patterns
low	low	low	1. Can't force people to drink it 2. Benefits extend to other age groups
low	low-moderate	high	1. Economic impacts—inability to get jobs or get to school may be high
low	moderate	high	1. Imposes difficulties on parents 2. Easier if there are waivers, but also less effective
low	low	low	1. No necessary impact on drunk driving
low	low	low	1. Gives teens an incentive to drive more safely; may have an impact beyond teen years
high	low	low-moderate	1. Expensive 2. Works best in tandem with other interventions 3. Difficult to keep in place
low	low	low	1. Little impact of penalties on behavior
high	high	?	1. Costly to develop and equip 2. Experience with seat belts not encouraging
low	low	low	1. No data on effectiveness, may be significant selection bias
low	low	low	1. No effectiveness over long term 2. Best in tandem with other interventions

Because of the centrality of the role of the automobile in our culture and the importance of drinking as a social institution, it is very difficult for our society to restrict either. The only group that can be targeted is young people below the age of twenty-one. However, the data show unequivocally that the twenty-one to twenty-four age group has a high fatality rate as a result of drunk driving. There has been no serious discussion of actions aimed at restricting this age group's access to drinking.

Although it is true that adolescents are more risk-prone than adults, which speaks to the appropriateness of delaying their access to a full license (to permit night driving) until they are eighteen or so, there is the countervailing element of skill. It is conceivable that delayed licenses might simply result in shifting the high rates of fatal accidents to the next-higher age group, twenty-one to twenty-four, which even now has a high accident rate.

Present efforts at community-wide consciousness raising, such as parental contracts, offer some prospect of reducing the high rates. It would be a mistake, however, to assume that they can have a substantial impact.

There is no easy way, really no way, of identifying prospectively the high-risk drivers. Accordingly, present knowledge and technology offer no reliable method of instituting effective deterrent programs. The costs of punitive programs also come very high and have extremely limited effectiveness. The major gains to date have resulted from improved safety on the roads over long periods of time. Nevertheless, alcohol-related accidents and deaths have come to loom ever larger as a percentage of total accidents and fatalities.

Society can only deal with drunk driving by exploring new approaches to reducing automobile fatalities. In this quest, we should not be bound to any one specific interventional approach, nor should we believe that a single program will provide a panacea. Drinking and driving are far too complex to assume that answers will come without a great deal of further trial and experimentation.

Notes

1. Ronald S. Karpf and Allan F. Williams, "Teenage Drivers and Motor Vehicle Deaths," *Accident Analysis and Prevention* 15 (1983):55–63.

2. Jack P. Desario and Frederic N. Bolotin, "A Sober Look at Drunken Driving Cure-All," *Wall Street Journal* 31 December 1985, p. 20.

3. Alexander C. Wagenaar, "Effects of the Raised Legal Drinking Age on Motor Vehicle Accidents in Michigan," *HSRI Research Review* January/February 1981.

4. Terry M. Klein, "The Effect of Raising the Minimum Legal Drinking Age on Traffic Accidents in the State of Maine," National Highway Traffic Safety Administration Technical Report, December 1981.

5. Delmas M. Maxwell, "Impact Analysis of the Raised Legal Drinking Age in Illinois," National Highway Traffic Safety Administration Technical Report, December 1981.

6. Allan F. Williams et al., "The Effect of Raising the Legal Minimum Drinking Age on Involvement in Fatal Crashes," *Journal of Legal Studies* 12(1983):169–179.

7. Desario and Bolotin, "A Sober Look at Drunken Driving."

8. Douglas Coate and Michael Grossman, "Effects of Alcoholic Beverage Prices and Legal Drinking Ages on Youth Alcohol Use," *National Bureau of Economic Research*, Working Paper 1852, March 1986.

9. Allan F. Williams et al., "Variations in Minimum Licensing Age and Fatal Motor Vehicle Crashes," *American Journal of Public Health* 73(1983):1401–1402.

10. Allan F. Williams, "Fatal Motor Vehicle Crashes Involving Teenagers," *Pediatrician* 12(1985):37–40.

11. Leon S. Robertson, "Patterns of Teenage Driver Involvement in Fatal Motor Vehicle Crashes: Implications for Policy Choices," *Journal of Health Politics, Policy and Law* 6 (1981):303–314.

12. Ibid.

13. H. Lawrence Ross, "Deterrence of the Drinking Driver: An International Survey," National Technical Information Service, March 1981:15.

14. Cited in Ross, "Deterrence of the Drinking Driver," p. 93.

15. Cited in Ross, "Deterrence of the Drinking Driver," p. 95.

16. Williams, "Fatal Motor Vehicle Crashes."

4

Teenage Pregnancy

Rising rates of teenage pregnancy and parenthood have become prominent factors on the nation's social agenda. The alarm was sounded dramatically with the publication in 1976 of *11 Million Teenagers—What Can Be Done About the Epidemic of Adolescent Pregnancies in the United States?*[1] Catapulted into action, Congress passed the Adolescent Health Services and Pregnancy Prevention Care Act (1978), and in the intervening years a wide array of public and private studies and service programs years have been directed at the categorical problems and needs precipitated by this trend. A 1986 report, *Teenage Pregnancy: 500,000 Births a Year but Few Tested Programs,* indicates by its very title the modesty of the accomplishments.[2]

The facts summarized in Table 4.1 are well known. Subaggregating the teenage female population into younger and older groups, we find that:

1. Among women aged fifteen to nineteen, pregnancy is increasingly prevalent. From a base of 95/1,000 in 1972 (the first year for which data are available), the rate increased to 111 in 1981 (the year of the most recent data), and there is evidence that the climb is continuing.

2. Teenage birthrates, like those for all women, have declined steadily and substantially, from 86/1,000 in 1952 to 62/1,000 in 1972 and to 52/1,000 in 1983. This decline is unevenly distributed: The rate for younger teenagers (fifteen to seventeen) decreased considerably less than that for women eighteen to nineteen, and the (minimal) rate for the youngest remained virtually unchanged. The actual rates (as of 1983) are 78/1,000 for women eighteen to nineteen; 32/1,000 for those fifteen to seventeen; and 1.1/1,000 for those younger than fifteen.

3. The birthrate for unmarried teenagers aged fifteen to nineteen increased from 23/1,000 (1972) to 29/1,000 (1982); the most recent (1983) estimate of live births to this group is 270,000 (30/1,000).

TABLE 4.1
Pregnancy and Fertility, Women Under Age Twenty

		Population (Women Under 20)	Pregnancies/ 1,000 (Women 15–19)	Births (in 000s)	Fertility/ 1,000	Percentage of Births Out of Wedlock (Women 15–19)
1960	Total	N.A.		594	89.9	14.8
	White			462	79.8	7.2
	Black			133	160.4	42.1
1972	Total	95		647	69.5	29.4
	White	—		468	57.9	17.1
	Black	—		179	152.9	62.8
1982	Total	111		524	54.0	50.7
	White	—		362	45.2	36.5
	Black	—		149	101.1	86.9

Sources: U.S. National Center for Health Statistics, *Vital Statistics of the United States,* annual, and unpublished data; U.S. General Accounting Office, *Teenage Pregnancy: 500,000 Births a Year but Few Tested Programs* (Washington, D.C.: GPO, 1986); and F. F. Furstenberg, Jr., J. Brooks-Gunn, and S. Philip Morgan, *Adolescent Mothers in Later Life* (Cambridge, Mass.: Cambridge University Press, forthcoming).

4. The difference between the pregnancy and fertility rates is accounted for primarily by abortions; about 45 percent of pregnancies terminate in abortion and some 5 to 6 percent in miscarriages.

A rising birthrate for unmarried teenagers is a particularly U.S. phenomenon. Although studies in the United Kingdom and other European countries have shown that, except for France, the trend toward increasing frequency of teenage, early teenage, and nonmarital pregnancy is not confined to any one nation, actual rates in the United States (even correcting for the disproportionate contribution of blacks) exceed those of all other developed countries. Fertility varies, however, among these countries depending on the availability of abortion. The extraordinarily high birthrates for U.S. black adolescents are approached only by those of the Arab population in Israel.[3]

Although in the United States intervention is perceived as urgently needed to control the rising number of teenage pregnancies and births, there is no consensus about the specific nature of the interventions, appropriate mechanisms, and an acceptable level of costs. That white teenagers are increasingly at risk of pregnancy has probably added to the importance of the issue among the dominant sector of the public.

Why Are Teenage Pregnancy
and Parenthood a Problem?

Besides the general perception in our society that because of immaturity, adolescent parenthood is suboptimal both for parent and for child(ren), what are the specific problems precipitated by early pregnancy and childbearing?

Teenage pregnancy is associated with leaving school before high school graduation. In an economy increasingly oriented to services, literacy, numerical skills, and similar competences, which require satisfactory completion of high school, are the basic minimum for employment in any but the most unskilled jobs, which are diminishing in number and which are being vigorously sought by new immigrants. The school dropout faces a foreclosure of opportunity for future economic security.

In the past, marriage—preferably before but if not, subsequent to the birth—was a workable solution to the social and economic problems of the unmarried mother and her child. Increasingly, however, teenage mothers are unwed and are remaining unmarried. Among black teenagers who give birth, about 90 percent are unmarried; the proportion among whites is about 35 percent (having risen from 7 percent in 1960 and 17 percent in 1970). The well-documented syndrome of female-headed family structure and poverty is a long-term threat to mother and child and to the public that bears the welfare costs of maintaining them. Additionally, the high probability of further pregnancies and births exacerbates the linkage with poverty.

The disproportionate number of births to unmarried teenagers among inner-city blacks is part of the complex of difficulties and disadvantages that affect this population. Forty-four percent (120,000) of the total of 270,000 births to unmarried teens in 1983 occurred in seven of the most populous states with large urban minorities.[4]

And finally, teenage births are associated with negative health conditions for mother and child and subsequent developmental difficulties for the child(ren).[5]

Although teen pregnancy and teen births are increasingly evident in the majority population, their disproportionate impact upon poor inner-city black communities has made this population the focus of concern and the target of remediation efforts; this discussion will be similarly focused.

If public policy is to be responsive to the negative sequelae of early births, just what should be targeted for prevention/intervention?

1. Precocious sexual activity?

2. Pregnancy (contraception)?
3. Births?
    Interruption of pregnancy?
    Avoidance of subsequent pregnancies?
4. Leaving school?
5. Dependency?

Although these are overlapping and frequently interrelated programmatic objectives, they differ in the commitment and often the constituencies they command. However, all involve influencing the personal choices and decisions of teenagers; unlike other sources of malperformance by the individual, there are almost no agents of change other than individual volition.

The best way to assess the potential for change may be to review the factors thought to be responsible for the dysfunctional choices made by teenagers and our inability thus far to alter them. Though many of these explanatory factors are at best hypotheses and there is some circularity of cause and effect, they provide an understanding of the context and the needs to which efforts at affecting changes in individual behavior must be responsive. They fall into the general categories of individual, developmental, cultural, social, and environmental factors.

To start with the underlying issue of precocious sexual activity, rates of sexual experience were estimated in 1979 to be 44 percent for white high school seniors (female) and 65 percent for those age nineteen; for black women, 73 percent at age seventeen and 89 percent at age nineteen.[6] By 1987, these figures are likely to be higher. They reflect the generalized sexual permissiveness of the dominant society, the heightened sexual orientation of the media and the culture generally, the ready availability of reliable contraceptive techniques, and, more recently, abortion to avoid unwanted births. Except for conservative religious groups, which have increased in visibility and militancy (their probably disproportionate influence on public policy will be noted), the authority of institutions that historically operated to maintain traditional sexual mores has diminished. Superimposed on the influence of the larger culture and the media are peer pressures for early sexuality. In the poor black community, early sexual initiation is not a new phenomenon, although it has been exacerbated in recent years.

With respect to the more problematic individual choices of unprotected sex, exposure to pregnancy, and the decision to complete the pregnancy and keep the child, a broader range of factors, endogenous and exogenous, are operative. Their relative importance as determinants is not well understood and probably varies considerably, certainly between younger and older adolescents. These include developmental factors such as immaturity (by definition), impulsiveness, susceptibility to peer influence, and rebelliousness against normative values and authority. Endogenous influences would include genetic characteristics such as poor intelligence as well as intrapsychic dynamics. Ignorance, misinformation, and community or peer mythology, particularly with respect to contraception and reproduction, also characterize the at-risk teenage population.

Teen pregnancy and parenting among inner-city girls are widely interpreted as an understandable response to the pathologic conditions of their environment. Limited current satisfactions, academic failure and boredom in malperforming schools, low self-esteem, and a pessimistic image of the future provide little incentive for deferring impulse gratification based on some calculus of future advantage.

The matriarchal structure of black family life and its greater tolerance of unmarried parenthood also cushion the stigma and the consequences of such births. For many girls, teenage pregnancy is an act of identification with their mothers. Others are following the example of their peers.

The welfare system is also thought to support the increasing trend of unmarried parenthood. It permits escape from the parental home and parental control, it lessens the importance of marriage and stable family formation for support, and it weakens the pressures for self-support.

These factors suggest that efforts to reverse the pattern of dysfunctional (by society's standards) sexual behavior must be geared to benefits that somehow satisfy the immediate needs of the teenager.

Programmatic Approaches

The vast array of efforts that have been mounted can be classified quite simply into two basic types: those directed to the prevention of pregnancy and those that provide assistance and services to women who are pregnant and/or mothers in order to avoid or ameliorate the negative consequences of teenage childbirth. Consistent with the overall social welfare tendency to corrective efforts after-the-fact, service programs for women who have become pregnant outnumber serious primary prevention efforts. In practice, there is considerable overlap with elements of both included in the service programs, which are mounted primarily by state and local sponsors. (The federal government occupies a very limited role in the direct program arena.) Secondary prevention is a focal component of all comprehensive programs directed at pregnant or parenting girls and is aimed at reducing further childbearing.

Within these large categories, programs vary by sponsor, type(s) of service provided, site of service delivery, population served, and scope of services. These differences reflect differences in public perceptions of appropriate goals, mechanisms, and agents of intervention, which may not be responsive or adequate to the needs and characteristics of the target population.

Primary Prevention

Primary prevention efforts range widely in their nature, content, and the mechanisms they employ. One can distinguish the purely educational (classroom instruction and discussion of sexuality and reproduction, often extending to family life, gender roles, and family planning); attitudinally oriented efforts (the inculcation and reinforcement of values, particularly in the area of interpersonal relations and group pressures, mostly through workshops, group discussions, etc.); parent-child communication; and contraception promotion, either in specific family-planning sites or in the context of general adolescent health care clinics.

It is fair to say that the vast majority of the U.S. public acknowledges the need for preventive efforts; nevertheless, the diversity of primary prevention programs speaks to differences in views of appropriate institutional roles and functions and the limits of intervention. A 1985 national survey revealed that 85 percent of adults consider teenage pregnancy a serious problem, which presumably the individual parent feels incapable of managing as 64 percent acknowledged having little or no control over their teenage children's sexual behavior. Nevertheless, the majority are reluctant to relinquish control over the information and the measures to which their children have access in the interest of preventing pregnancy and would specifically limit the availability of contraceptive services without their approval.[7]

The most universal technique is school-based sex education. Beyond the obvious statistical evidence that such instruction has not succeeded in reducing the pregnancy rate, the more important finding may be that neither is there evidence that it has *encouraged* sexual activity. Fear that this would occur has been an important rationalization of those opposed to the introduction of sex education into the classroom.

When it comes to programs explicitly geared to the knowledge and persistent use of reliable contraceptive methods, almost all types that have been studied can report *some* positive results. These include school-based or school-linked clinics that provide contraceptive services; family planning clinics that enroll teenagers; and comprehensive clinics, both school-based and hospital-based. However, confidence in these outcomes is limited because they are, for the most part, short-term—some programs have not been followed for a sufficient period, in others initial reductions in pregnancy or births relative to comparison groups have faded over time. In 1987, there is no *conclusive* evidence pointing to the greater effectiveness of any particular type of program, and in those programs that have shown positive results, the particular (or sets of) characteristics or services that are responsible have not been identified.

Illustrative of the more promising efforts at primary prevention is a recent project designed and executed over a period of four years by researchers from the Johns Hopkins departments of pediatrics and OB/ GYN in cooperation with the administrators of four inner-city schools in Baltimore, two junior high and two senior high (one of each served as a control).[8] At the experimental sites, the state-mandated basic sex education curriculum was supplemented with a school-based counseling and information service staffed by an on-site social worker and a nurse practitioner or midwife. These same professionals also provided medical services as well as group and individual counseling and education in a close-by clinic. Both programs were available daily and all medical services were free. The population served was exclusively black and predominantly of low socioeconomic status. A built-in evaluation component, based on periodic surveys of both experimental and control students, indicated positive changes in knowledge, attitudes, and sexual behavior over a period of two and one-half years of exposure to the program. There was a striking increase in clinic attendance and pill use, particularly among younger students; low incidence of failure to use any contraceptive method; and a brief postponement of seven months of first coital experience (from age 15 years 7 months to 16 years 2 months), which was noteworthy given the prevailing high rates of sexual activity among the population of the study schools. Although initially pregnancy rates were not favorably affected, after prolonged experience with the program there was a drop in the incidence of conception; this was particularly impressive when compared to a striking rise among the control groups.

Perhaps the most important outcome of this project is not the quantification of its accomplishments but the tentative identification of the relevant factors. The evaluators concluded that (1) accessibility of the staff and the clinic and continuity of services are more effective than any "new" information provided to adolescents; (2) attitudinal changes are very difficult to achieve, therefore, greater improvement may be expected from reinforcement of those already holding positive attitudes and helping them to translate these attitudes into constructive behavior than from attempting to influence those who do not share these views; and (3) early program exposure is important before teenagers develop behavior patterns that place them at risk of pregnancy. It is essential to evaluate rigorously the implications of the Baltimore program in other locations, to identify the characteristics of the populations and the environments for which it will work, and to isolate the program components that lead to positive results.

Services to Pregnant
and Parenting Teenagers

Services for teenagers who have become pregnant preempt the bulk of current programmatic efforts. Except for abortion services, which we will discuss separately, these programs may be categorized by objective and focus, which include health and well-being (of mother and child), prevention of subsequent pregnancies, and education and employment. Like the prevention efforts that have been described, success of the latter two efforts is contingent upon influencing choices made by teenagers. The payoff for them, however, is remote in contrast to their immediate personal needs, desires, and experiences, and frequently conflicts with the environmental norms and pressures to which they are exposed.

School Programs

The one agency that has a mandatory responsibility for the pregnant teenager is the school. Title IX of the National Education Act (1972 amendment) affirmed that pregnant students have the same rights to education as all other students, which effectively prohibited the then customary practice of the schools—expulsion or exclusion from classes. It did not require schools, however, to provide special programs for pregnant adolescents.

Some perspective on the dominant role of the school may be gained from reviewing the funding sources for teen pregnancy programs. With the federal effort limited to just one program that serves pregnant teenagers exclusively (the Adolescent Family Life program) and several others that target or are relevant to them (such as family planning, employment and job training, the Supplemental Food Program for Women, Infants, and Children [WIC], health and social services), states and localities provide most of the expenditures. At these levels, program support for pregnant teenagers comes overwhelmingly from education departments. Faced with the dilemma of permitting the student to remain in a normal classroom (less costly but also far less acceptable to the community and frequently unattractive to the student) or setting up special programs, most schools in both conservative and liberal communities have opted for the latter. To the extent that these programs recruit from the school population, they clearly miss those who have dropped out or who are only marginally attached to school by virtue of poor performance and are most deprived educationally. There are a variety of models with regard to site (off-campus or within the regular school); duration (pregnancy or pregnancy and postpregnancy); focus (preparation for childbearing and parenthood along with some academic maintenance or academic advancement to motivate the student to continue her education after delivery); and the scope and quality of the services and staff. A 1981 Rand Corporation study found that no one model could be universally advocated since success of any program depended on its fit with the environment—community attitudes, incidence of pregnancy, and the concentration or dispersion of the student population.[9]

In principle, however, relatively few school systems have responded with constructive, positive programs that realistically integrate the specific needs of the pregnant and parenting teenager and educational objectives through the provision of appropriate supports and adjustments. School administrators and staff rarely fill in the service gaps that are inherent in their particular program model. These gaps are wide-ranging and include transportation needs; sensitivity to the student's conflict and/ or incapacity to cope with her situation; need for flexibility in school procedures, requirements and standards; health requirements; the need for infant care; and so forth. All of these factors militate against achievement of their primary objective—to maintain school attendance. At this juncture in her life, the pregnant teenager is not preoccupied with school and school achievement. In the case of those who have persevered steadfastly and successfully to graduation, their retention may be attributed as much to unusual individual motivation as to the presence of the program. It seems obvious, moreover, that school graduation alone, although it meets formal programmatic objectives, offers no clue to the achievement of more fundamental and long-range goals, i.e., avoidance of further pregnancy and childbearing, effective educational achievement and skill acquisition, and self-support.

It is within this generally dismal context that a few promising school program models have been developed that have the common characteristic of being noncurricularly oriented. They are essentially oriented toward services that are of immediate need to the individual. They provide counseling, referral to community agencies for assistance during and after pregnancy, tutoring, and medical care (including contraceptive services) through on-site clinics or links with close-by health facilities. Services continue well past delivery. Judged by quality standards, these programs rank high; however, reliable comparative outcome data are not generally available, and there is little follow-up of the student's subsequent career.

The exemplary Johns Hopkins–Baltimore project that has been described is one of the limited number of intensive and imaginative attempts to deal with primary prevention in a school-setting, which goes beyond the short-term educational requirements of the state.

Comprehensive Programs

In contrast to primary prevention programs, and implicitly as a means of finessing the controversial issues inherent in a direct preventive approach, a comprehensive services model was promoted in the 1970s as a preferred intervention to address the newly emerged problem of teenage pregnancy. This approach links educational, social, and health services for teenagers and is essentially a variant of the large-scale programs developed by the federal government during the preceding decade to address social problems through services. The rationale for these programs lay in the initial studies conducted largely upon populations of inner-city blacks, which showed a relationship between teenage parenthood and the catena of health deficits (for mother and child), welfare dependency, and school leaving. Accordingly, federal policies favored the establishment at the local level of comprehensive packages that included a variety of services supported by multiple funding streams. Serious concern about teenage pregnancy arose, however, at about the time that confidence in large service programs had begun to wane, and as a result, aside from its intrinsic flaws, the comprehensive approach has suffered from very limited federal funding. Direct federal support for services to pregnant teenagers goes to a relatively few demonstration programs; most programs operate under the aegis of state education or social welfare departments and utilize as ingeniously as they can federal health, education, vocation, and welfare funding not designed explicitly for this population.

The essential components of a comprehensive program are generally considered to be health services (prenatal and postnatal) including contraceptive services; social services and counseling, particularly with reference to sexuality, reproductive behavior, and family life; and education and vocational training. Although these services all address problems that characterize the major portion of pregnant teenagers (poor urban minorities), there is little empirical evidence suggesting their efficacy in preventing subsequent pregnancy(ies). Furthermore, by definition, they exclude the population that could conceivably be assisted to avoid this particular pathology in the first place. To the extent that they are successful, these programs are useful in ameliorating some of the sequelae of teen pregnancy, but they have no impact on its cause and cannot be considered preventive. Aside from being "too late," most are also "too little" in the sense that they are focused on the period of pregnancy and services terminate with delivery, after which the teenager is left to negotiate the problems and demands of youthful parenthood without programmatic assistance. Hence even the opportunity for secondary prevention (i.e., prevention of subsequent pregnancy) is not exploited. It must be noted that this bleak appraisal of the potential of comprehensive programs overlooks a number of exemplary demonstrations that have been undertaken. These have extended contact with the teenager into the postdelivery period when supports with the long-term role and tasks of parenthood may have greater influence upon the adolescent's subsequent behavior.

Although local sponsorship enhances public support for programs, optimizes the use of available resources, and tailors content and structure to local needs, it is frequently a source of weakness in that available resources are frequently in inverse proportion to need, content, administration, and public support, and are unduly subject to extremist political influence.

Adolescent Family Life Programs

The Adolescent Family Life Act (AFL) of 1981 and the projects that it has funded are the Reagan administration's response to the problem, which, to quote its sponsors, "will only be answered by the resolve of . . . families, communities, churches, synagogues. . . ." The program is committed to the principle that control of teenage pregnancies and births can and should be achieved through the deferment of sexual activity, a value to be conveyed privately by parents and traditional moral authorities. In the event of an unwanted pregnancy, adoption is almost the only feasible alternative. The program has funded demonstrations, which are distributed nationwide and not especially targeted to urban or to poor populations. If one disregards the program's premises and its inviolable conditions, the AFL program is structured to resemble older, more mainstream programs and follows a comprehensive approach. It has the same dual focus: prevention and care. The family is heavily involved, and there is an explicit attempt to reach adolescent boys as well, both in the effort to postpone sexual activity and in the support services provided during pregnancy and after delivery. The chief distinguishing feature of the effort is that contraception and abortion are unconditionally interdicted.

Because the earliest AFL demonstrations have not been in progress very long, there have been only interim reports and no summary evaluations, although evaluation is an integral component of each project. It is hard to make an informed judgment of these programs that is not tinged by one's subjective biases with respect to the fundamental approach. Nevertheless, the core components of the programs must provide a useful service to many teenagers in helping them cope with the tasks of early parenthood and in maintaining their own health and that of the child. Many of these are familiar: counseling, day care, education, parenting skills, nutrition, etc. Because these components have appealed to teenagers in the context of other more liberal programs, there is no reason to expect any lesser utilization and effectiveness here. Their conservative premises may also be helpful in overcoming parental resistance toward assuming a positive role in dealing with the immediate problems of the pregnant teenager. A priori, one can assume that the emphasis on deferred sexual activity can reinforce the behavior of those teenagers who are sympathetic to it in the first place, but under the growing pressures favoring early sexuality, it is unlikely to affect seriously the larger urban population at risk.

Societal Attitudes and Parental Practice

We now turn our attention from the adolescents whose choices and behavior pose the problems, but who have no input into remedial policies or programmatic solutions, to the adult public whose responses alone matter. One cannot underestimate the influence of the profound ambivalence of U.S. society to the current impasse. Conservative standards (uncertain at best) with respect to sexual issues as well as personal inhibitions about becoming involved in this area of adolescent development and behavior have pervaded the search for a solution at every level of intervention. By way of illustration we consider intrafamilial parental practice and parental involvement in programmatic efforts.

Intrafamilial practice. Much has been made of the centrality of the family in the genesis of the child's value structure, particularly in the area of interpersonal relations and morality. Applied to sexual behavior, this would imply that the parent should take active responsibility for the child's instruction and guidance, and in fact the issue of public/private interest and authority is a continuing item in the public policy debate. Going further, parental participation has been widely proposed as a necessary component of programs to teach and influence teenagers, particularly in the effective use of contraception. The evidence seems to be, however, that parents avoid any serious commitment to this role. Surveys indicate that though a large majority of parents report having spoken with their children about sex (median age ten at first occasion), it is a fairly superficial stab at the real problem, and the topic of birth control is infrequently discussed. Thus the model of open, frank, and informative communication with their children that most adults believe to be their essential contribution to avoiding teen pregnancy is in real life the exception rather than the rule and must reflect an inner ambivalence on the part of parents toward pragmatic steps that might conflict with deeply held moral values. One can only infer that adults fear involvement might represent complicity in their children's sexual activity, which they would prefer were deferred and which they certainly do not want to appear to condone. This discomfort with the issue must be clearly conveyed to their children who report that they characteristically receive and share information (and misinformation) and advice with siblings and peers in preference to adults. The inhibitory effects upon pragmatic measures of the public/private responsibility dilemma are reinforced by the underlying preferences of most parents to avoid the issue(s).

Programmatic involvement. The potential of parental involvement has also been adopted by many preventive programs that encourage mother-daughter discussions, often in a group setting, and maternal knowledge and support of birth control services. However, adolescent girls have not reported a high degree of success in talking comfortably with their mothers about sex and birth control, nor much improvement in compliance with contraception.

Despite the recognition of their own inadequacy, a large proportion of parents wish to maintain control (or the illusion of it) over their children's sexual education. This is reflected in conflict over the content of school programs (though parents overwhelmingly favor the inclusion of sex education in the curriculum) and more particularly in the measure of support (about 50 percent) for the so-called "squeal law," mandatory parental notification of a teenager's utilization of contraception services (even though parents do support mandatory links of school programs with family planning clinics).

Abortion

Abortion is the most divisive of all the issues relating to teenage pregnancy. Clearly, abortion falls outside the rubric of prevention, except in a secondary sense, although it may be argued that the availability of this service may be thought of by some as fallback prevention that reduces the urgency of primary contraceptive practice. Even discounting the powerful antiabortion sentiment of Catholics and conservative/ fundamentalist Protestants, pro-choice support at the present time is weakening. Strength of the opposition varies with the measure by which it is gauged; that is, surveys indicate that opposition to a constitutional ban on abortion has been reduced to slightly over 55 percent and support for *Roe v. Wade* stands at 50 percent. In light of the mounting concern over teenage births this suggests the limits to which the public is willing to go to prevent it. Although it is not likely that *Roe v. Wade* will be repealed, neither can widespread expansion and generalized availability of abortion services be anticipated as a mechanism to control teenage fertility.

The depth of the controversy over abortion and the extent to which normally nonpolitical actors and mechanisms are being engaged may be inferred from a story that appeared in the *New York Times* headed "Madonna's New Beat is a Hit, But Song's Message Rankles".[10] Although it is hard to claim that the hit pop song "Papa Don't Preach," was inspired, its message to teenagers and their parents seems to be clear that abortion is more reprehensible than an illegitimate birth and that romantic love attenuates the stigma of pregnancy. This is remarkable on two accounts: Sexual morality is not the normal fare of popular songs, in fact it has been assiduously avoided, and the conclusion resembles the views current in the White House.

All told, these issues reveal a society in conflict with respect to the liberalized sexual climate of the past two decades, which reflects itself in the contradictions between the expressed need to avoid the pathologies that have emerged, particularly as they affect youth, and the adoption and serious pursuit of pragmatic actions at both personal and public levels.

Conclusions

With the availability of reliable contraceptive techniques, priority should be given to interventions aimed at primary *prevention*, i.e., protection against pregnancy. Not only would this be the stratagem of least cost (immediately and surely in the long run), but it would also be consonant with the expressed views of the majority of the U.S. public. Concern by the majority population for protection of their own teenage children may generate support for comparable efforts for the poor adolescent population. This is not to deny or minimize the current ambivalence and confusion of society with respect to the instrumentality of birth control: the appropriate locus of authority, the preferred agency, the role of the parent, alternative route(s), mechanisms, and value systems. Nevertheless, the probably permanent change in normative sexual behavior in the nation underscores the urgency and the potential for sex education and contraceptive instruction. Serious efforts at clarifying the confusion and accommodating conflicts in public perceptions would seem to be a necessary component or precondition for a significant prevention commitment.

Intuitively, the school would seem to be the agency of choice to assume this responsibility. The school system alone has universal authority over the youth population that is both mandated by law and accepted by society. To the extent that it misses (or loses) those adolescents who have dropped out or are only tenuously attached to school (and who may conceivably be at greater risk than the large majority of their peers), supplementary institutions would clearly have to be involved.

The search for effective interventions is seriously compromised by the scarcity of knowledge about the determinants of individual adolescent behavior. In-depth research into the differential motivation patterns of young women in the area of sexual behavior is needed for the design of programs and mechanisms to which they will be responsive. Much of this understanding can be derived from the experience of programs in progress, particularly those that have shown some signs of success. Identification and analysis of the differences between those who have benefited and those for whom the program has failed and the reasons (not the rationalizations) for success or failure, are important in tailoring and refining effective approaches.

The overall paucity of positive outcomes from the programs that have been mounted may be attributed largely to their characteristically short-term horizon. To alter the behavior of individuals, particularly during adolescence (a period that by definition is marked by ongoing change, volatility, and immaturity), requires more intensive, surely lengthier effort (at the very least reinforcement and follow-up) than most programs permit. This may be an explanation for the "fade" phenomenon observed in many initially successful efforts. Stabilization of desired outcomes in this population may be contingent upon long-term contact.

The absence of longitudinal studies of teenage cohorts as they grow older leaves us seriously deficient in any understanding of either the long-term consequences of programmatic interventions or the effects of earlier sexual and reproductive behavior on their subsequent lives. As it is the adult experience of adolescents that is our ultimate concern, it is essential to have the data by which to judge the validity of the assumptions underlying programmatic interventions as well as the consequences of those interventions. The updating and adaptation to the current adolescent population of Frank Furstenberg's studies begun more than a generation ago are an urgent priority.[11]

Most programs are hybrids and combine a mixture of components that may be offered in fixed or variable patterns to the population served. Evaluative efforts, however, even if performed with proper comparison groups, rarely examine the contribution of individual program components and combinations of components to success or failure. More typically program outcomes are related to characteristics of the individual, producing an estimate of who benefits from the overall program, and are assessed by qualitative and quantitative criteria. For purposes of program refinement, institutionalization, and replicability, rigorous analysis is required to identify just which elements work, which are ineffective, and which may be counterproductive.

Given the influence of the adverse socioeconomic conditions under which urban minority teenagers grow up and in particular the poor outlook for adult life upon motivation in the area of sexual/reproductive behavior, efforts that create realistic alternative career options (diplomas and jobs) would seem essential for any basic change in their calculus of the importance and advantage of avoiding early pregnancy.

At the present time, despite reports of positive results by a variety of programs, there is very little information on the effectiveness of projects either specifically for the prevention of initial pregnancy or of more comprehensive services targeted to the reduction of subsequent pregnancies, ensuring maternal and child health, or encouraging return to school and achievement of self-support. The brighter side of the news is that there is some receptiveness to experimentation with innovative approaches. These, however, should be designed on the basis of deeper knowledge of the teen population, should be continued for a far longer period than has been the case in the past, and should be conducted with rigorous concomitant evaluation and follow-up.

Notes

1. Alan Guttmacher Institute, *11 Million Teenagers—What Can Be Done About the Epidemic of Adolescent Pregnancies in the United States* (New York: Planned Parenthood Federation of America, 1976).

2. U.S. General Accounting Office, *Teenage Pregnancy: 500,000 Births a Year but Few Tested Programs* (Washington, D.C.: GPO, July 1986).

3. C. S. Chilman, "Some Psychosocial Aspects of Adolescent Sexual and Contraceptive Behavior in a Changing American Society," in J. B. Lancaster and B. A. Hamburg, eds., *School Age Pregnancy and Parenthood: Biosocial Dimensions* (New York: Aldine De Gruyter, 1986).

4. GAO, *Teenage Pregnancy.*

5. T. Field, S. Widmayer, S. Stoller, and M. de Cubas, "School-Age Parenthood in Different Ethnic Groups and Family Constellations: Effects on Infant Development," in Lancaster and Hamburg, eds., *School Age Pregnancy.*

6. Chilman, "Some Psychosocial Aspects."

7. Louis Harris and Associates, "Public Attitudes About Sex Education, Family Planning, and Abortion in the United States," conducted for Planned Parenthood Federation of America, Study No. 854005, August–September 1985, unpublished.

8. L. S. Zabin, H. B. Hirsch, E. A. Smith et al., "Evaluation of a Pregnancy Prevention Program for Urban Teenagers," *Family Planning Perspectives* 18(3):119–126.

9. G. Zelman, *The Response of Schools to Teenage Pregnancy and Parenthood* (Santa Monica, Calif.: Rand Corporation, 1981).

10. Georgia Dullea, "Madonna's New Beat Is a Hit, But Song's Message Rankles," *New York Times*, September 18, 1986, p. B1.

11. F. F. Furstenberg, Jr., J. Brooks-Gunn, and S. Philip Moran, *Adolescent Mothers in Later Life* (Cambridge, Mass.: Cambridge University Press, forthcoming).

5

Drug Users

The results of the most recent national survey of illicit drug use in the United States reveal that 37 million Americans above the age of twelve (or about one in five people) admit to having used drugs within the last year.[1] About one in ten admit to using illicit drugs in the month just prior to the survey. These data, along with increased media attention generated by the recent drug-related deaths of sport celebrities, have catapulted the drug use issue into national prominence and given the problem a renewed importance on the public's agenda.

Signs of the resurgence of public concern about drug use are omnipresent. The president (and first lady) crusade for mandatory drug testing for federal employees; Congress has shown its willingness to ignore the provisions of the Gramm-Rudman spending limitations bill in its attempt to deal with the problem; candidates for political office vie with each other as to who is the toughest on drugs; the media acclaim children who turn their parents into the police for drug use; and celebrities who publicly denounce drug use (even their own) are the lions of television and radio talk shows.

Much attention has been devoted to the problem of adolescent and preadolescent drug use, but much of this concern appears exaggerated. The most recent surveys have shown with few exceptions a continued decline since the mid-1970s in adolescent drug use. The most important exception is a slight increase in the number of adolescents aged twelve to seventeen who report they have used cocaine within the last year, up from 4.1 percent in 1982 to 4.4 percent in 1985. However, 44 percent of the adolescents who reported using cocaine, used it in the form of crack, a more potent and potentially more addictive substance that is smoked rather than snorted. Adolescent use of alcohol also increased between 1982 (26.9 percent of teens reported using it within the month prior to the survey) and 1985 (31 percent). Both figures are below the 1979 reported monthly use rate of 37 percent.

TABLE 5.1
Drug Use in the United States, 1982

	Percentage Using Drugs in Past Month (according to age)			Total Number of Users, All Ages (in millions)	
	12–17	18–25	>25	Past Month	Past Year
Alcohol	26.9	67.9	56.7	100.2	124.7
Cigarettes	14.7	39.5	34.6	60.2	69.6
Marijuana	11.5	27.4	6.6	20.0	31.5
Cocaine	1.6	6.8	1.2	4.2	11.9
Hallucinogens	1.4	1.7	<.5	1.0	4.1
Heroin	2.5	<.5	<.5	<1	<1
Stimulants	2.6	4.7	0.6	2.9	7.0
Sedatives	1.3	2.6	<.5	1.6	5.5
Tranquilizers	0.9	1.6	<.5	1.1	4.1

Source: National Institute on Drug Abuse, *Household Surveys* (Washington, D.C.: GPO, 1982).

It should be noted that surveys of self-reported drug use yield questionable results. The survey noted above explicitly excludes populations living on military bases, in jails, dormitories, and institutions, as well as the homeless and runaway populations. Because it is likely that use among these groups may be higher than the average, the overall survey statistics are probably low. Moreover, although the survey statistics show that drug use is endemic in the United States, they do not speak to the degree of usage, which might give a better sense of the extent of drug use.

Table 5.1 gives utilization data based on the 1982 survey of U.S. drug use. (The most recent survey data from 1985 have not been published in detail.) Except for alcohol and cigarettes, the rates described in the table are for illicit drugs that have not been medically prescribed. It is clear from Table 5.1 that drugs are consumed in inverse proportion to their perceived danger. Thus heroin and hallucinogens are used far less frequently than alcohol, cigarettes, and marijuana.

The concerns about adolescent drug use are twofold: (1) excessive drug use can result in health problems in later life, and (2) excessive use of drugs can lead to ineffective performance and reduce the life opportunities of young people.

Even though cigarette use in the United States has declined over the past several years in the face of mounting public pressure to eliminate cigarette advertisements and to ban smoking in public areas, adolescent women have been least affected by this trend. There is concern that

TABLE 5.2
Drug-Related Deaths Reported to DAWN System, 1981

	All Ages	Ages 10—17
Narcotics	1,360	13
Sedatives	1,084	26
Tranquilizers	421	4
Amphetamines	186	3
Hallucinogens	84	1
Cocaine	84	1
Marijuana	9	3
Total	3,228	51 (1.6%)

Source: DAWN Annual Report, 1981.

the overall number of teenagers who are developing early drinking problems has increased, and, as noted above, more teens are using cocaine in its most addictive form.

There are few serious health outcomes from the social use of drugs (except over the long term), as reflected in reports from the Drug Abuse Warning Network (DAWN). The DAWN system includes 819 emergency rooms in twenty-six metropolitan areas as well as randomly selected nonmetropolitan counties around the country. In addition, DAWN also receives reports of drug-related deaths from a sample of eighty-four county medical examiners and coroners. Table 5.2 documents the fatalities related to drug abuse from a sample of eighty-four county medical examiners and coroners. The data in Table 5.3 are based on emergency room visits in which drug abuse was the precipitating cause of the visit.

It must be noted, however, that Table 5.2 excludes deaths related to alcohol (such as alcohol-induced driving fatalities, a particular problem among teenagers). It should also be noted that a large portion of these fatalities result from suicide attempts, particularly those involving the use of tranquilizers. The data in Table 5.3 do not justify excessive concern about the immediate health impact on teenagers of drug abuse, particularly those drugs whose use has evoked the most media attention. The more important concern is the effect of drug use on future adolescent behavior and the ability of adolescents to prepare for and lead a productive life. Even in this area, or perhaps especially in this area, public and media confusion have exaggerated the impact of adolescent drug use.

Drug use, by all age groups, exists along a continuum (depicted in Figure 5.1) from nonuse at one pole to heavy use (addiction, dependence) at the other. Each step on the continuum is discrete. However, taking

TABLE 5.3
Drug-Related Emergencies Reported to DAWN System, 1981

	All Ages		Ages 10–17	
	Number	Percent of Total	Number	Percent of Total
Sedatives	24,179	27.0	2,131	27.8
Tranquilizers	23,769	26.5	1,759	22.9
Narcotics	20,067	22.4	679	8.8
Amphetamines	6,082	6.8	942	12.3
Hallucinogens	5,884	6.5	1,079	14.0
Cocaine	4,777	5.3	158	2.0
Marijuana	4,671	5.2	906	11.8
Total	89,429		7,654	

Source: DAWN Annual Report, 1981.

into account the array of drugs available, an individual may find him or herself at a different step along the continuum for each substance.

Nonuse means that a person has never tried a particular drug or abstains from drug use completely. Experimental use indicates that a person has used a particular drug or drugs once or twice but not more than that. Recreational or social use refers to those who take drugs in particular settings or only at particular times. Habitual users utilize a drug or drugs on a regular basis (as opposed to the occasional social event). Heavy users are people who are dependent on a particular drug or drugs—addicts. Clearly, the ideal social goal is to keep everyone close to the left of this continuum; for those people who are on the far right of the continuum, the object is to help them shift back to the left. Except for cigarettes, few people, particularly teenagers, go beyond recreational use for most drugs.

Several issues need to be addressed in order to clear up much of the confusion surrounding heavy drug use. Physical dependence is a condition

FIGURE 5.1
Continuum of Drug Use

Nonuse——experimental use——recreational/——habitual use——heavy use
                                         social use

Source: Adapted from J. M. Polich, P. L. Ellickson, P. Reuter, and J. P. Kahan, *Strategies for Controlling Adolescent Drug Use* (Santa Monica, Calif.: Rand Corporation, February 1984).

in which the body has adapted to the presence of a drug and undergoes a withdrawal syndrome when the use of that drug is reduced or stopped. Withdrawal syndromes vary widely among different drugs from the mild to the severe, but in general withdrawal is not nearly as strenuous or difficult as is typically portrayed. For some drugs, dependence is more psychological than physiological, and withdrawal syndromes tend to present psychological symptoms rather than physical ones.

A third form of dependence is an increasing tolerance for a drug so that the body requires larger, more frequent, or more potent doses to produce the same effect. In order to get a "high" increased quantities of the substance are required.

All forms of dependence come from frequent use of a drug over a relatively long period of time (weeks or months). People do not become addicted from one or two experiments with a substance, and usually recreational drug use does not lead to dependence. Only sustained and regular use of a drug will lead to dependence, even in the case of narcotics.

A possible exception to this general principle may be found in so-called "designer drugs," where the potency is so high that dependence is achieved very rapidly. Designer drugs are controlled substances that have been slightly modified on a molecular level and therefore may be purchased legally. In many cases, alterations in the structure of the drugs vastly increases their strength and effect. There are, however, no scientific or rigorous studies of such drugs and most data are anecdotal.[2] Moreover, these substances tend to have a relatively limited attraction, and by the time they achieve even a modicum of publicity, they are generally labeled as dangerous drugs and their purchase is prohibited. Because of their cost (generally high), they are not a significant factor in adolescent drug use.

Although illicit drug use has received the most media attention, it is clear from Table 5.1 that cigarettes and alcohol are the drugs of choice for teenagers. Because of their ready availability and low price, it is far easier for an adolescent to become a regular or heavy user of alcohol or cigarettes than of other drugs. As noted above, with the exception of cocaine, aggregate adolescent use of illicit drugs seems to be declining.

Types of Drugs and Their Use

Narcotic Drugs

Narcotic drugs (heroin, morphine, opium, codeine) and synthetic narcotics (dilaudid, demerol, darvon, methadone) produce sleep and reduce pain. They are "hard drugs" usually taken by intravenous injection (or by pill in the case of the synthetics). Of all the drugs, narcotics tend to produce the most severe physiological dependence (addiction), and tolerance builds up quickly requiring increased quantities and frequency of use. Most of the negative health outcomes from narcotics are attributed to sequelae of administration rather than to the drugs themselves (e.g., AIDS, hepatitis, and bacterial infections from the use of nonsterile needles).

The stereotypes of narcotic use are also mostly incorrect. Addiction comes only after frequent use of the drugs for several weeks or more (and emphatically not from a single injection), and detoxification (by complete, immediate withdrawal) is generally not nearly as painful as *Man with the Golden Arm* movies would suggest. A single fix of heroin may cost $20 to $30, and addicts may require two or three fixes a day. As a narcotic, heroin produces a sleepy dreaminess in its users. However, the need to ensure enough money for the next fix leads to a great number of street and property crimes.

The development of methadone was initially perceived as a means of controlling some of the negative outcomes of narcotic use, such as the need for intravenous shooting-up and the need to raise money to supply the ever-increasing quantity of the desired drug. Methadone prevented the withdrawal symptoms associated with heroin but didn't require injection; if given to addicts, it would eliminate the need to resort to crime to support their drug habit. Although methadone does accomplish these goals, it does so outside of the social milieu that is an important ritual in drug use. As a result, many drug users in methadone maintenance programs continue to use other drugs as well.

Of all the different types of drugs, narcotics are the least used by adolescents (and others as well). The recent association of intravenous (IV) drug use with AIDS and other serious diseases has prompted renewed educational attempts to get users to use sterile needles so that these problems can be reduced. According to estimates, there are 200,000 IV drug users in New York City (out of about 500,000 in the United States), and they are predominantly found in black and Hispanic communities.

Cocaine

The emergence of cocaine as a problem drug for adolescents is a recent phenomenon. Cocaine as a stimulant has always been an expensive drug. With a gram of cocaine (typically enough for one or two people for several hours) costing between $75 and $100, it has always been a drug for the affluent. It was also held to be a relatively harmless drug in terms of its physiological effects. Newer methods of use (smoking) and more potent methods of administration (free-basing) have allowed for lower prices, stronger effects, and a rash of cocaine-related fatalities (most notably, that of Len Bias, the University of Maryland basketball star). Although the price of cocaine is still high enough so that normally only the affluent can afford enough to become habitual users, there has been increasing use of cocaine by teenagers, particularly in the form of crack. Crack costs only $5 to $10 per use; it is therefore affordable to first-time or recreational users. However, addicts may resort to street and property crimes to support their habit.

Marijuana

Its relatively innocuous side-effects, its low price, and the social and euphoric state it produces make marijuana the illicit drug of choice among adolescents and the most widely used illicit drug in the United States. Recent surveys have shown regular (habitual) marijuana use to be decreasing among adolescents and even among older people. The heavy use of marijuana in the 1960s and 1970s led many cities and states to decriminalize its possession but not its sale, although the ability to grow marijuana in almost any environment renders supply-side controls ineffective. The real fear associated with marijuana is that after experimenting with its use, adolescents will begin to use other, harder illicit drugs as well. Although it is rare for teens to begin to use harder drugs without having tried marijuana first, there is no causal domino-like connection that automatically leads from marijuana to other drugs.

Hallucinogens

Hallucinogenic drugs including LSD, PCP, mescaline, and others became popular in the late 1960s. Their use has been diminishing since then. They are rarely taken on a regular basis, and there is conflicting evidence about their health effects. Because many of the hallucinogens are made in home labs, the user never knows exactly what is being ingested.

Stimulants

The main illicit stimulant drugs are amphetamines and their derivatives. Although caffeine is the most frequently used stimulant, its use is not considered to be a serious adolescent problem. Amphetamines have two actions that make them attractive: They energize people and keep them awake, and they suppress the appetite and can be used as dieting aids. Because of these characteristics, stimulants are widely used by adolescents, primarily by college students. As dieting aids, stimulants are widely available through prescription and are also easily made in home laboratories. Crackdowns on overprescription by physicians has significantly reduced the use of amphetamines, but they have made a comeback as drugs for hyperkinetic children (idiosyncratically slowing them down). Heavy users of amphetamines may begin to inject the drug intravenously, and the effects of the high doses together with the hazards associated with needle use can lead to significant health problems.

Sedatives

Sedatives are drugs used to induce sleep. The major sedatives are barbiturates. Nonbarbiturate sedatives include Quaalude and Placidyl. Sedatives are frequently used in adolescent suicide attempts (almost 50 percent of adolescent deaths caused by sedatives are suicides). The effects of sedatives are intensified by the use of alcohol, and a large number of motor vehicle accidents result from combinations of sedatives and drinking. Sedative use seems to have peaked in the late 1970s (particularly Quaalude use) and to have leveled off since then.

Tranquilizers

Tranquilizers are antianxiety drugs and are the most widely prescribed drugs in the United States. Dependence on tranquilizers is harder to achieve than dependence on sedatives; tranquilizers also tend to have fewer severe physical effects. However, the psychological dependency caused by tranquilizers may be greater.

Alcohol

Because it is used most frequently by many teenagers, alcohol is the most serious drug discussed in this chapter. The dangers of teenage drunk driving have been discussed previously, but it should be emphasized that over 6,000 teens die yearly in alcohol-related motor vehicle accidents. Because alcohol (though a controlled sale substance) is so widely available and so cheap, it is the easiest drug for teenagers to use. Ready availability and the large numbers who drink alcohol make the potential for alcohol abuse quite high.

Cigarettes

Of all the drugs discussed, cigarettes create the greatest health problems as large numbers of adolescents smoke. Even though smoking among adolescents has dropped significantly over the past ten years (the rate for teenage boys declined from 28 percent to 16 percent; for teen girls from 28.8 percent to 20.5 percent),[3] cigarettes remain for teenagers the second most used drug, after alcohol. Moreover, the transition from

FIGURE 5.2
Points of Intervention

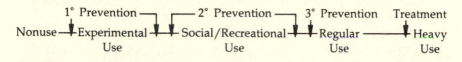

Source: Adapted from J. M. Polich, P. L. Ellickson, P. Reuter, and J. P. Kahan, *Strategies for Controlling Adolescent Drug Use* (Santa Monica, Calif.: Rand Corporation, February 1984).

experimental use to heavy use occurs far more quickly with cigarettes than with other drugs, with consequent long-term health implications.

A recent source of concern has been the growing use of smokeless (chewing) tobacco among teenagers. The substance was originally marketed on the premise that its health impacts were considerably less severe than those of cigarettes as the tobacco was chewed rather than inhaled. Recent studies have found the substance to be not much less noxious than cigarettes, and recent campaigns have been started to discourage the use of smokeless tobacco.

Thus, the major drugs that adolescents use are the restricted legal drugs (alcohol, tobacco) rather than the illicit ones.

Methods of Prevention

Given the continuum of drug use, it is possible to locate particular points of interventional opportunity. Figure 5.2 identifies the points on the continuum where preventive and treatment activities could take place.

Primary prevention is focused on keeping adolescents from experimenting with drugs or, if they have already tried drugs, keeping them from becoming more frequent users. Primary prevention programs address the universe of adolescents as all teenagers are at risk of beginning use of drugs.

Secondary prevention programs seek to keep social/recreational users from becoming regular or heavy users. Many programs focus on youth who are considered to be at high risk of becoming more frequent users. Tertiary prevention programs are similar to secondary prevention efforts but narrow their focus to those who have already manifested or exhibited some problems resulting from or related to drug use. These symptoms might include absenteeism, learning difficulties, delinquency, or health problems. In general these programs avoid teenagers who are identified as heavy users (i.e., are already physiologically or psychologically drug dependent), but in many cases the distinctions are not sharply drawn.

Treatment programs focus on adolescents who are exhibiting clearly dysfunctional behavior and whose use of drugs is more habitual and extensive.

It should be noted that the distinctions between prevention and treatment may overlap, depending on the type of program and the number of users it seeks to address.

Primary Prevention Programs

Because school-based antidrug use programs have been ongoing since the mid-1960s, a considerable amount of knowledge has been accumulated about these programs and their effects. Although few of these programs have been rigorously evaluated, it is possible to draw useful conclusions about adolescent drug use patterns. This section draws heavily on a study performed by the Rand Corporation for the Conrad Hilton Foundation.

Historically, different programs have been established for different drugs. Alcohol programs have been separate from smoking programs, which have been different from marijuana and other drug programs. In part this has been due to separate sources of funding, but also because the use of different drugs has differing antecedent causes and therefore different approaches to prevention are needed.

In terms of use and impact, prevention efforts should be targeted at cigarette smoking, alcohol use, and marijuana use, as these are the drugs of choice of adolescents. Yet, each of these drugs is used differently by teenagers. By age twelve to thirteen, less than 2 to 3 percent of teens have used marijuana or smoked cigarettes. By age sixteen, 20 to 30 percent of teens use marijuana or smoke cigarettes. Thus prevention programs that start in junior high school have the possibility of preventing over 95 percent of teens from smoking or using marijuana.[4] (There is a danger, however, that starting at an earlier age brings with it the possibility of encouraging experimentation rather than preventing it.) Yet by age twelve to thirteen, over 10 percent of adolescents have been drinking alcohol.[5] Therefore it would make sense to start alcohol programs earlier than antismoking or antidrug programs. Moreover, the work of Eric Kandel and associates at Columbia have shown a sequential (though not causal) relation between use of legal drugs (alcohol, cigarettes) followed by marijuana, followed by harder drugs.[6] It has been postulated that if the use of alcohol and cigarettes is prevented (or delayed), the use of other drugs may be prevented or delayed as well. In fact there is no systematic research on the spillover impact of prevention against one form of drug use on other drugs.

Primary prevention for adolescent drug users has been accomplished typically through mass media programs and through school-based programs. There is no evidence that mass media programs and public service advertising have any effect on drug use, although it is known that "fear" messages are less effective than general educational messages. School-based programs can be categorized according to the following four types:

1. The oldest and most prevalent programs use the "information model." Programs such as these assume that teenagers need information about drugs in order to make informed choices. The programs may be conducted by teachers or guidance counselors or by outside experts. The programs may be once-a-year lectures or continuing parts of the curriculum throughout the year. Evaluations of these types of programs show that they are effective in increasing the amount of information adolescents have about drugs, but there is little evidence that knowing more about drugs actually has an impact on use. That is, knowledge does not necessarily affect behavior.

2. The "individual deficiency model" postulates that adolescents use drugs because they lack self-esteem. The programs use various value clarification techniques to try and build up the adolescent's sense of himself or herself. These programs, like the information programs, also differ greatly in their format and content. Evaluations of these programs are inconclusive, but it seems reasonable to assume that it would be difficult for these programs to change in a few hours a self-concept that is the product of the adolescent's entire life. Perhaps even more important is the fact that there is little hard evidence of any relationship between self-image and drug use.

3. The "alternatives model" assumes that one reason that teenagers use drugs is that they lack other outlets—a "devil makes work for idle hands" approach. Programs that adopt this approach attempt to find socially useful (and remunerative) projects for teens to engage in during after-school hours. Some of these programs emphasize after-school employment and career development. To date there have been no evaluations of the effectiveness of these programs.

4. The "social pressures model" is one that has become increasingly popular since the late 1970s. This model attempts to counter the impact of peer pressure as a factor leading to the use of drugs through programs that teach adolescents skills and offer support for rejecting peer pressure and saying "no." These programs are more effective when the message is delivered by other teenagers. Many use teen-sponsored drug-free clubs and social events to implement this strategy. In several studies this model has shown a significant impact in reducing the number of teens who smoked cigarettes compared with a matched control group.

Although these programs have been effective against cigarette smoking, there are no evaluations as to their effect on preventing or delaying the use of other drugs. The significance of this lies in the fact that there has been a secular decrease in cigarette smoking among all ages; the hazards of cigarette smoking are daily reported and trumpeted on television, and local antismoking ordinances (in over 150 municipalities across the county) have given further emphasis to an antismoking sentiment. Thus, even though this approach holds promise, there is no assurance of its effectiveness in curtailing adolescent use of other drugs. It should also be noted that the evaluations of these programs have not examined whether there is any substitution effect; that is, although fewer teens use cigarettes, have they shifted to using other drugs?

Secondary and Tertiary Prevention

The major difference between programs of secondary and tertiary prevention and the primary prevention programs described above is that the former are not aimed at the universe of adolescents, but rather at those who are considered to be at high risk of drug use or who have already acknowledged drug use. Although programs of this type are generally composites of primary prevention programs, the emphasis of each program differs widely. In New York City, for example, the secondary and tertiary prevention programs focus on "saying no" with less attention devoted to value clarification and information. A major risk with programs of this sort is that they may serve to forge a new peer group of drug users, which will make it more difficult to deter use.

Treatment Options

In general, treatment options for illict drugs can be broken down into four basic approaches: (1) detoxification, (2) methadone maintenance, (3) therapeutic communities, and (4) drug-free programs. Alcohol and smoking abatement programs are structured differently and are not addressed. The illicit drug treatment programs can be defined as follows.

Detoxification is a medical treatment of supervised withdrawal from a particular drug. As a strictly medical procedure (although social supports may be available), detox does not deal with larger psychosocial or economic dynamics of drug use. Detox is used primarily for those drugs that produce a strong physiological dependence (narcotics, alcohol) rather than for drugs that produce a more psychological dependence.

Methadone maintenance is a form of narcotic addiction therapy in which a synthetic drug is substituted for the more dangerous initial substance (usually heroin). The advantages of methadone are (1) it is given orally and thus eliminates the use of needles; (2) it does not produce a narcotic high; (3) it blocks the effects of other narcotics taken during treatment; and (4) it lasts longer than heroin. Thus a heroin user enrolled in a methadone program no longer has to buy an illegal drug (thereby reducing crime) and no longer has to inject himself (thereby improving health). Methadone maintenance is useful only for narcotic abusers and not for other drug abusers.

Therapeutic communities are residential treatment centers in which the drug user is sheltered from external pressures while he or she tries to become drug free. The community provides a mutual support group for drug users as they attempt to become resocialized without the use of drugs.

A drug-free program is the generic term for all other typically used treatments that are noninstitutional, nonresidential, and do not provide alternative drugs. The different strategies used in this modality include: (1) behavioral therapies—biofeedback, hypnosis, aversion therapy; (2) psychotherapy and counseling; and (3) crisis intervention—hot lines, walk-in centers, referral centers, crash pads.

The basic problem with most of the treatment programs described above is that they use heroin-abuse treatment as their model. However effective or ineffective these programs may be for heroin abuse (and they are largely ineffective), they are totally inappropriate for adolescents and the drugs adolescents use.

Adolescent drug users generally do not enter drug treatment programs of their own volition. They are either forced to enter or do so only in order to avoid a prison sentence. Consequently, there is little motivation for adolescents to respond favorably to such programs. Because so few adolescents are heroin abusers, programs based on this model are likely to be ineffective. Not only do they stigmatize the youth who are placed in programs of this type, but they may also push teenagers into harder drug use. The treatment modalities described above treat drug use as either a physiological or psychological problem, and their basic thrust is to stop the addiction. Adolescent drug use, to the extent it can be defined at all, seems to have its roots in interpersonal and intergenerational problems. As such, these treatment modalities are inappropriate for most adolescents.

The evaluations of treatment programs are methodologically weaker than those of prevention programs. There is no randomization of treatment modality, nor are there control groups or post-treatment follow-up. Clearly much more research is needed to devise more effective treatment programs.

Programs to Interdict Drug Use

The United States has a long history of attempts to interdict drug use through deterrence and criminal prosecution. These efforts have fallen short of reaching even the minimal goals set for them. A basic reason for this is that most people do not equate using drugs as a crime of equal gravity with robbery, rape, or murder. A second reason is the vast profit to be made through the sale of drugs. A prime example of the failure of drug interdiction policies can be seen in the recent attempts to stop cocaine from entering the country and, once it has entered, to keep it from being sold.

When the United States used economic pressures to obtain the cooperation of the Turkish government in stopping the production of opium in that country (which was estimated to be 80 percent of the opium that found its way to the United States), opium producers shifted their operations to Mexico. Within two years, Mexico was exporting the same amount of opium into the United States as Turkey had two years earlier. The situation with cocaine is somewhat different, as it is only grown in three Latin American countries (Peru, Bolivia, Colombia), and it is uncertain the substance can be grown in other countries. It has not been possible to secure sustained government cooperation to reduce cocaine output in these countries for several reasons: (1) cocaine is grown in jungle areas where there is only minimal government presence; (2) it would be extremely expensive to substitute another crop for cocaine because of the high economic return cocaine brings; (3) the cocaine growers and their distributors have formed their own private armies to protect their areas; and (4) it is likely that government and army leaders receive substantial economic rewards for inaction.

The real profits from the sale of cocaine accrue once it gets to the United States. Despite massive attempts to control its importation, there has been little progress in this area. Cocaine powder, in the form of small bricks, is easy to smuggle, and the potential profits create a large supply of people willing to take the risk of carrying the substance across borders. Increasing efforts to stop the importation would be extraordinarily expensive and probably of limited utility. Moreover, because the price of cocaine rises so much once it has entered the United States, increased interdiction of shipments would have only a minor impact on retail prices. Rand corporation researchers estimate that if the interdiction rate was to rise to 40 percent of shipped cocaine (from the estimated 20 percent), the retail price would increase only 3.4 percent.[7]

Police attempts to restrict sales at the retail level have been no more effective. The penalties for sale are too small and the profits to be made too great to have a substantial impact. Cocaine retailing is thought to be done less by individuals and more by organized groups of sellers who have substantial economic resources to buy off local police and the legal resources to mitigate the outcomes of cases that go to trial.

It is difficult to overstate the amount of money to be made through the retail sale of illicit drugs. A 1983 study by Abt Associates estimated that there were between 500,000 and 1.3 million marijuana dealers in the United States earning between $5,000 and $15,000 from that activity.[8]

For adolescents, the prospects of high incomes with limited risk is great. Even if a teenage drug dealer is caught, it is likely that he or she would be treated as a minor and suffer no or minimal incarceration. Even if teen dealers do not use drugs themselves, as is frequently the case, they have access to other adolescents, which allows these dealers to make a significant profit. The accoutrements of drug profits—expensive clothes, tickets to rock concerts, expensive cars, jewelry, and so forth—are a clear indication that high school education or graduation is not a requirement for the good life. With the job prospects for inner-city teens bleak and with only minimum wage and dead-end jobs as real alternatives, the allure of a windfall income (for an adolescent) and a fast life-style through the underground economy is increased.

In summary, increased law enforcement measures, even if successful would have only a marginal impact on the price or supply of drugs in the United States. It should be noted that the situation for other illegal drugs differs in that few are as geographically concentrated in source of origin as cocaine.

Conclusions

The aim of adolescent drug use programs is to prevent teenagers from using drugs or to delay their use. Contrary to the current media-generated controversy over adolescent drug use, the drugs that teenagers use most frequently are alcohol, cigarettes, and marijuana. Cocaine use, although increasing, is still a minor problem, and harder drugs are even less frequently used.

Despite the fact that drug programs of various types have been in operation for more than twenty years, there is still little objective evidence about the effectiveness of these programs. To date, only anticigarette smoking programs have had any success, and this has happened in the context of nationwide attempts that encourage everyone to stop smoking. It is possible that programs that do not target adolescents specifically may be effective for teens by not singling them out as a group. To the extent that adolescents are emulating adults, programs that get adults to stop using drugs may also help teens.

We also need to learn more about the effects of drug prevention programs targeted to a particular drug on the use of other drugs and on other adolescent social problems. The value clarification and peer influence skills that are taught in drug use prevention programs are generic. They should influence adolescent behavior in such areas as teenage sexual relations and unsafe automobile driving habits. Whether these spillover effects occur, and what mechanisms can be employed to coordinate programs directed at teen behavior should be explored. There is a need to coordinate the variously funded programs addressed to different issues or different approaches. For example, further research is necessary to evaluate the effectiveness of antidrug programs that are combined with adolescent employment and job training programs.

The possibility that exaggerated attention placed on teenage drug use may in fact lead to greater drug use also should be evaluated.

It would be unrealistic to expect that all adolescents will either not begin to use drugs or delay their use until they had achieved a maturity that would allow for safer use. It should be possible, though, to develop programs that will allow teenagers to make rational choices based on accurate information. Given the ineffectiveness of drug interdiction policies, both on the supply and demand side, and the inappropriateness of treatment programs, the best choice is for the development of more effective prevention programs.

Notes

1. Joel Brinkley, "Drug Use Held Most Stable or Lower," *New York Times*, 10 October 1986, p. A14.

2. Winifred Gallagher, "The Looming Menace of Designer Drugs," *Discover*, August 1986, pp. 24–35.

3. "10-Year Study Says Number of Smokers Fell by Almost 20%," *New York Times*, 20 October 1986, p. A18.

4. J. M. Polich et al., *Strategies for Controlling Adolescent Drug Use* (Santa Monica, Calif.: Rand Corporation, February 1984), p. 121.

5. Polich et al., *Strategies*, p. 123.

6. D. B. Kandel, "Stages in Adolescent Involvement in Drug Use," *Science* 190 (1975):912–914.

7. Polich et al., *Strategies*, p. 67.

8. K. Carlson et al., *Unreported Taxable Income from Selected Illegal Activities* (Cambridge, Mass.: Abt Associates Inc., 1983).

6

School Dropouts

My interest in youth unemployment goes back to my academic studies at Heidelberg University in 1928 and 1929. It was clear to me at the time that Nazism was attracting unemployed university graduates, many of whom concluded that they had nothing to lose by joining a political party that promised, among other things, to provide jobs for all. On the basis of this early exposure, I have postulated that only a society that is willing to jeopardize its future will tolerate large and continuing unemployment among young people who can so easily provide the ammunition for social explosion.

In World War II, the U.S. Armed Forces encountered a serious manpower problem because over one million young men of draft age were unable to pass the requisite fifth grade literacy test. In South Carolina, 1 of every 4 black selectees failed the test, while in the Northwest, the failure rate was only 1 of 100 white males. Because of the thinning supply of selectees, the army inducted about 300,000 illiterate men and placed them in special units that were commissioned to bring the recruits up to a minimum level of literacy. I have detailed this experience in *The Uneducated.*[1] I also followed up these recruits after military service and warned that because of the decreasing opportunities for unskilled laborers on farms, poorly educated U.S. citizens would find it increasingly difficult to obtain the jobs that would permit them to maintain themselves and their families.

On the positive side, the World War II experience demonstrated that intensive second-chance opportunities could make a difference if the individuals were motivated to acquire the competency that was necessary for military service. Hard as it is for many to believe today, in 1942 and 1943 young men wanted to serve in the army.

The Negro Potential detailed the markedly lower investment that our society had made in the education of black versus white youth, and the extent to which this underinvestment together with labor market discrimination reduced the opportunities available to blacks in the nonagricultural sectors of the economy other than at the lowest rungs of the occupational ladder.[2] Very few industrial jobs were open to black men in the South except in blast furnaces and sawmills—two of the most disagreeable types of physical labor.

The last chapter of *The Negro Potential* noted, however, that discrimination in the labor market was beginning to yield, particularly in the North, and one of the challenges that the opening of opportunities presented was the speed with which blacks would be able to improve their educational qualifications in order to take advantage of these new jobs and career opportunities.

In 1971, the Twentieth Century Fund sponsored a task force on the unemployment of black youth. The following quotation from its report, *The Job Crisis for Black Youth*, pinpoints how little has changed in the past fifteen years:

> It is only at the gravest peril to our society that American people continue to ignore the growing frustration, despair, and hostility that characterize, more and more, young black people. After a childhood and adolescence stunted by deprivation, rejection, and neglect, these young people want the opportunity to support themselves and to live useful lives. But, as reports of the Equal Employment Opportunity Commission and other government agencies underscore, many desirable training and employment opportunities remain closed to black youth.
>
> Many black young people have grown up in households with only one natural parent. They have lived in slum housing in slum neighborhoods where violence and crime are commonplace. They have attended schools where teachers do not teach them, where the curriculum is irrelevant, and where there are no performance standards. The family that should have nurtured them, the school that should have instructed them, the community that should have opened opportunities for them, the democratic society whose professed faith should have encouraged them—all have failed. They reach adulthood with one basic achievement not to be despised: they have survived their environment.
>
> What they most need is a second chance to find themselves, to fit into a society that, through neglect—or worse—has seriously handicapped them. If there are walls they cannot scale that keep them out of jobs or confine them to the drudgery of ill-paid dead end work, then they are doomed to live permanently as marginal workers, to exist forever on welfare, to dwell in the twilight zone of illegal employment or to exist as criminals in and out of prison. A society that turns its back on them invites only the enmity of the young and puts its own future in grave jeopardy.[3]

In 1978, two black graduate students at the Columbia University School of Social Work undertook a study of the views of two groups of black youngsters in Harlem toward their schools, education, and career goals. The report, *Tell Me About Your School*, published by the National Commission for Employment Policy, highlighted the following: For the most part, the younger group (ten- to eleven-year olds) found their schooling a positive experience while the older group (fourteen- to fifteen-year olds) found it largely negative.[4] The disorder in the schools—including risks to life and limb, physical and emotional intimidation, the inability and unwillingness of many teachers to make a serious effort at teaching, the lack of any relationship between what was occurring in school and the student's future prospects—created a dysfunctional environment. Most pupils saw no reason to stay and earn a diploma because they knew of no one who had obtained a decent job as a result of graduating from high school.

From 1962 to 1981, I served six presidents as chair of the successive national advisory committees that oversaw the expenditure of about $100 billion for employment and training programs, a considerable portion of which was directed toward assisting youth. The most important conclusions from this unique experience are set out below.

1. There was no broad support in Washington for a program modeled on the Civilian Conservation Corps (CCC) of the depression years, even though Senator Hubert Humphrey was a leading advocate of such an effort. My interpretation is that in the 1930s Congress saw youth unemployment as a national issue since it affected both whites and blacks; by the 1960s and 1970s, unemployment was less pervasive—it primarily affected blacks and Hispanics.

2. Trade unions were not hospitable toward federal programs to facilitate the entrance of youth into the labor market until the late 1960s when almost all of their adult members had been reemployed.

3. Congress was willing, especially after the Watts riots, to spend money to keep young people "quiet" over the summer vacation by giving them so-called work with wages. However, Congress never was disposed to fashion a serious youth employment program except for the Job Corps, in which enrollment was always constrained.

4. The Job Corps was seriously designed and executed. It was targeted at the most disadvantaged. It also was comprehensive in that it provided for educational remediation, skill acquisition, and, most important, linkage, upon completion, to some constructive next step such as military service, an approved apprenticeship program, or return to school. Moreover, initially Congress was willing to underwrite an exclusively residential program. It must be noted that although this feature proved beneficial to some, the program was not an overwhelming success because a high proportion of enrollees (two out of three) failed to adjust to the new environment and withdrew long before the end of the year.

In 1977, fifteen years into the federal training effort, Congress passed a series of youth employment programs, one of which was an entitlement effort. In a limited number of cities and counties, all young people, both in and out of school, who met the screening criteria (low family income) were entitled to participate in a school/work program that had three basic objectives: to increase the proportion who would complete the course and obtain their high school diplomas; to encourage dropouts to return to school and do the same; and to enable both groups through work experience to obtain jobs (and better jobs with more pay) once they entered the labor market full time.

The Manpower Demonstration Research Corporation (of which I am chairman emeritus and an active board member) was awarded a contract to evaluate the program. My reading of the results is that the program was less successful than would have been anticipated: The school retention rate revealed only small gains as a result of summer jobs and part-time employment during the school year; the return to school by dropouts was negligible and the employment/income gains of the participants once they entered the labor market were limited. The most important outcome of the entitlement effort was the ability of the program to locate sensible jobs for the young participants and the employers' generally positive experience with the enrollees.

It should be stressed that the program suffered from its quick launching and early demise, as did most other federal efforts. It is hard to know whether more favorable results could have been obtained if the program had had a longer life, if there had been time for adjustments, and if some of the strengths at one project site could have been replicated at others.

Within a year of the program's commencement, the favorable Congressional attitude toward employment and training efforts for adults as well as for youth had peaked and turned downward. The chief architect of the youth bill, Representative Ronald Sarasin of Connecticut, believed that even before Congress had acted on his bill, the principal goals had been distorted and weakened.

A few additional observations: The federal effort put dollars on the barrel-head, which were then apportioned to more than 100 prime contractors, to the states, and to a limited number of national organizations (National Urban League, Opportunities Industrialization Centers, and so forth). Aside from simple accounting and financial controls, once funds were parceled out, the federal government had little opportunity to influence the structure and functioning of specific program efforts. There was great variability in how programs were carried out, reflecting differences in the macro-environment, the competence of the contractors, and the extent to which efforts focused on or ignored the most disadvantaged.

There also was considerable variability in the extent to which the training programs were able to elicit the interest and support of the school systems as well as what was done with the money set aside for a school's discretionary use. It is fair to say that the linkage between the employment and training programs and the school systems was, with few exceptions, poor or nonexistent.

Although in 1976 Congress became interested in targeting federal funds to the most disadvantaged groups in the community, and although states and prime contractors moved over time to respond, there was continuing resistance by program operators to doing so because of the difficulties inherent in training seriously handicapped individuals in the educational competences and the socialization skills needed to make them job-ready. As most program administrators want to point to successes, not failures, they look to enroll persons who are most likely to succeed.

Two contemporaneous observations: The currently in-force federally funded Job Partnership Training Act (JPTA), which contains an allocation of 40 percent for youth, has encountered repeated difficulties in spending its full allocation because under federal criteria contractors are assessed on the basis of the proportion of trainees that successfully enter the job market. Many of the most disadvantaged youths are poor bets and therefore are not enrolled in JPTA. To make matters worse, JPTA does not pay stipends or wages, and has relatively little money for the support services needed by many young women for child care and other assistance.

In the June 1986 issue of the *Journal of Economic Literature*, there is a contribution by Albert Rees (president of the Sloan Foundation and one of the nation's most astute observers of labor markets) entitled "An Essay on Youth Joblessness."[5] The following quotations from his summary bear directly on this analysis:

> The United States government has been pursuing policies to reduce youth joblessness, especially among black youth, for more than 20 years. Despite these policies, the problem has been growing worse. (p. 624).
> The core of the problem of youth joblessness is the problem of the youth who do not complete high school. (p. 626)

In an earlier section headed, "The Black Youth Joblessness Puzzle," Rees observes

> Finally, the difference in employment rates by race . . . could be one element of a syndrome that includes a high concentration of poverty,

substandard housing, female-headed households, high rates of teen-age pregnancy, drug use, crime. We see clearly that the racial differences in youth unemployment are very large and understand only dimly why. (p. 623)

Quoting a 1986 National Bureau of Economic Research report by W. Kip Viscusi, Rees notes that one in five youth admitted to "some illegal activity in the year preceding the survey . . . most often . . . selling drugs and illegal gambling such as 'numbers.' The total may be greatly understated particularly because very few of the respondents admitted to more serious crimes such as mugging or burglary" (p. 623).

This retrospective can be summed as follows:

1. Unemployment among black youth has been worsening over the years.
2. The federal government has in the past directed considerable sums to its alleviation but has achieved only modest success.
3. Unemployment is a critical problem for high school dropouts.
4. Joblessness is probably only one aspect of the wider array of ghetto pathology.
5. Our understanding of the causes of youth unemployment is limited and, as Rees stresses in light of past federal efforts, "It is not easy to suggest policy options for the years ahead" (p. 624).

Framework and Parameters

I agree strongly with the thrust of Rees' analysis and differ only with respect to his modesty as to what we know and whether, in light of the earlier shortfalls in federal efforts, we are able to design effective devices for intervention. In late 1987, my conceptualization of the problem–a precondition to identifying potentially useful intervention devices—follows:

1. The U.S. public school has always been a more effective instrument for middle-class than for poor youngsters, white or black.

2. Much of what the school takes credit for by way of instruction and education takes place in the family. To quote the observation of the former rector of the University of Amsterdam about the experience of the early postwar years: "We were confronted with a new challenge: formerly, students had been educated at the table of their parents, but this was no longer true once admissions were opened to young people from the lower social classes."

3. Whether the youngster takes school seriously is dependent on whether parents and other influential figures encourage, support, and

insist on behavior that is proschool rather than antischool or indifferent to school.

4. The quality of the school—general atmosphere, peers, teachers, and administrators—is an important factor in outcome (see James Coleman's studies[6]). Racially segregated neighborhoods almost ensure that the environment of the school will be dysfunctional, especially because the public school is a school of last resort. Parochial schools can transfer out unruly youngsters, but not so public schools.

5. Many middle-class black families who are making it (approximately one-third of the black population in a northern state) relocate out of the ghetto as soon as they can; if they do not, they are likely to send their youngsters to private or parochial schools, which means that the public school population is reduced to the lowest possible denominator with respect to social class and diversity.

6. In large cities, where most blacks and Hispanics live, teacher unions have strong influence on the assignment process so that the youngest, least experienced teachers usually are assigned to the most difficult ghetto schools.

7. A major responsibility of the administrators of ghetto schools is to ensure the physical safety of pupils and staff, which is no small task if recorded violent incidents are taken as a first indicator of the problem. Keeping order in the classroom and in the school definitely and understandably takes precedence over teaching.

8. For the reasons already enumerated, and others that could easily be added (for example, the fact that many pupils lack sufficient sleep and nutrition to be attentive and responsive in the classroom), many ghetto youngsters begin early to fall behind in the acquisition of basic competences, particularly reading and mathematical skills.

9. As was pointed out in *Tell Me About Your School*, with a few youngsters accelerating, some keeping pace, but with many falling behind in effective learning and some being kept back, the age and skill span tends to widen to a point where it is very difficult for the teacher to instruct seriously or for the receptive pupil to learn something new because the majority of the class is not ready to absorb new material.

10. Given these and many other intractable problems, a large number of teachers, after trying to cope, give up, which sets the stage for even less learning on the part of students.

11. It is a great mistake to assume that youngsters exposed to this type of school do not catch on that the entire enterprise is marked by a basic unreality: No one is really interested in teaching them; the classroom is dysfunctional even when the instructor is interested in teaching; avoiding conflicts with the dominant students—often older boys who have been left back—is an essential first challenge to teachers;

nothing or very little that happens is satisfying to the pupils; and the entire process will not pay off, so why bother.

12. Coming from families in which only the rare individual has a regular job that pays enough to support its members, these youngsters fail to make a connection between what is occurring in the classroom and how acquiring competences might pay off when they are ready to find work.

13. To make matters worse, their egos have been adversely affected by their awareness that U.S. society holds blacks and Hispanics in low esteem. And, as noted earlier, they often do not have the "demonstration effect" of blacks who have used the school/work nexus to find a way out.

14. As anyone who walks around New York City can attest, although youngsters may report to school at starting time, many can be found on the streets after 10 AM, looking for something to fill their time, anything rather than confront the boredom of the classroom. Some do not bother to come to school at all (truancy technically defined), many others are escapees from school for most of the day. Some may return at lunchtime, but others do not.

If these observations are a reasonable first approximation of the present situation in most ghetto schools—and I believe that they are— then it must be evident that effective interventions will not come easily and surely not inexpensively.

A Catena of Intervention Efforts

As a transition to the concluding section about new directions for intervention, a brief schematized overview is presented below.

The past two decades have seen significant net, real dollar additions to the budgets of all school systems including substantial allocations to ghetto schools. The only sensible conclusion to be drawn from this experience is to point out that money alone—although it may help at the margin by increasing the number of paraprofessionals, providing sports subsidies, and underwriting some special events—has not noticeably improved student outcomes.

The same conclusion must be reached when it comes to radical administrative changes such as placing considerable responsibility in the hands of community boards, which, at least in New York City, has failed to lead to significant improvements.

For the most part, the push toward "alternative schools" seems to have petered out, although not without leaving some signs of strength in a number of communities such as Philadelphia, where they really took root.

There is scattered evidence to suggest that the infusion of new teaching talent in the late 1960s from among the civil rights activist and anti-Vietnam cohort was a positive short-term benefit for the pupils who were exposed to them. But most of these newcomers left teaching after a few years.

In many cities, including New York, there have been successful efforts at establishing close, supportive ties between large corporations and "adopted" schools. Corporate adoption often leads to additional resources, human and financial, for the school. Some youngsters gain a more realistic view of the world of work, and the best students have opportunities to work part-time or full-time over the summer. I designed and oversaw a multiyear project for Citibank and the Martin Luther King, Jr. High School. It was not easy to operate and it was not cheap, but it had worthwhile payoffs for the participants. An unexpected dividend was the interest of Citibank's middle managers who felt good about their involvement.

Although the federal entitlement program referred to earlier had a modest effect on the school retention/graduation nexus, it offered some work experience and income, particularly income, to young enrollees. Most cooperative programs, however, have been highly selective, offering opportunities to pupils who were better, not worse, than average.

Recently, there have been some efforts in Los Angeles, California, and Dallas, Texas, to lengthen the school year to eleven months or so in order to cope with overcrowding and to determine whether lengthening the school year can result in more effective learning. It is much too early to reach even a tentative judgment about the potential of this innovation.

There have been useful volunteer programs directed at tutoring ghetto school children. New York City has a sizable program as do a considerable number of other cities.

There are various opportunities available to high school dropouts to secure a GED (high school diploma equivalent) usually through military service, employer special efforts, local school districts, and junior colleges.

The foregoing does not pretend to provide an inclusive list of interventional efforts or even a close approximation. All that it has sought to do is to indicate the range and variety of efforts that have been undertaken in the past, most of which are still being pursued, to shore up in one way or another the conventional public school system, which in recent years has graduated only from 40 to 60 percent of its minority cohort.

FIGURE 6.1
Behavior-Intervention Matrix

	Dropouts	Youth Unemployment
Specific Programs		
Process Improvements		
Macro-Changes		
Second-Chance Opportunities		

New and Strengthened Interventions

This concluding section will make use of the behavior intervention schema developed in Chapter 2, which distinguished among program, process, macro-, and second-chance interventions, with a focus on school dropouts and youth unemployment (see Figure 6.1).

One can readily recognize that for the most part prior interventions to reduce the dropout rate have centered on programs to strengthen the performance of school systems on the assumption that if this occurred student retention would improve. The principal emphasis of interventions to reduce youth unemployment has been on employment and training programs to provide unemployed and underemployed youth with work experience and first-order skills in the belief that after such exposure beneficiaries would be better positioned to obtain and hold a regular job.

As noted earlier, the outcomes of prior intervention devices leave a great deal to be desired in that the dropout rate among low-income, inner-city groups, especially minorities, remains excessively high; and in the face of significant federal government efforts, at least in the second half of the 1970s, the youth unemployment trend for this population has worsened, not improved.

The schema outlined above helps to clarify that in programs to reduce both the dropout and youth unemployment rates, the other major lines of intervention—process improvements, macro changes, and second-chance opportunities—although not totally neglected, have been relatively underemphasized.

The remainder of this chapter will consider briefly new or strengthened intervention devices that hold promise of contributing to either or both of the stipulated goals—a lower dropout rate or lower unemployment for youth—along each of the four axes (programs, process, macro changes, and second chance). Special emphasis will be placed on the latter three because, among other reasons, they have been relatively underexplored in the past. Major efforts currently under way along these four axes will be reviewed and attention directed to their specific strengths and weaknesses. This section will consider the school dropout issue first, jobs for youth second, and conclude with a few observations on the relationship between the two.

Interventions for Dropouts

There is a growing consensus among many groups that are committed to strengthening the public school system that high priority should be given to programs aimed at raising teachers' salaries—recommendations that are often linked to "merit" performance, recertification, national qualifications, and so forth. It would be hard to argue against the desirability of such efforts as the prevailing pay scale is, with relatively few exceptions, insufficient to attract and hold the average college graduate, not to mention those with above-average qualifications and training. But it is questionable whether salary reform can be introduced on a significant scale, quickly enough, to make a real difference in the performance capabilities of ghetto schools.

Recently, the executive director of the Chief State School Officers observe that most chief officers have not concentrated in the past on the acute problems of inner-city schools, but they are beginning to recognize the need to do so. Among the high priority issues that he identified was the need to attract more minorities into teaching, which he thought could be done by better articulation among junior colleges, senior colleges, and special state funding to assist interested and capable minority students. Chicago has an embryonic program under way.

A related approach that draws heavily on the comparative success of private schools in replenishing their teaching staffs with young college graduates would be for the public school system to aim deliberately at short-term recruitment (say for periods of three to five years, by establishing links with teacher training programs) and to provide young teachers sufficient freedom for experimentation. These and other attractions and rewards could serve as a lure. For instance, upon completion of a three- to five-year contract the young instructor might be entitled to a year of subsidized graduate study or some comparable remuneration.

A third type of program could build on existing volunteer tutoring efforts. Such a program could be broadened, deepened, and provided with supports such as pupil transportation.

Still another approach would be to devolve more responsibility from the central school administration to the principal. Recognizing the special problems that inner-city schools face, state and city boards of education should be encouraged to allocate a modest fund (5 to 10 percent of their annual appropriations) to principals for their discretionary use.

The foregoing programs—more minority teachers, the recruitment of young teachers, term contracts, and more freedom and resources for principals—are not offered as solutions but as potential program interventions that hold some promise of having a positive impact.

Clearly, all program interventions will be limited if one believes that the dropout phenomenon is the result of multiple and cumulative flaws in a developmental process in which the decision of the adolescent to drop out is only the final step. A process approach requires that one explore how the cumulative failure could be reduced and in many cases eliminated.

Advocates of the Headstart program maintain that proper orientation to school in the preschool years will act as a long-term preventive against later dropout. Even though there are scattered studies that point in this direction, many able developmental psychologists such as Jerome Kagan remain unconvinced. A priori, the thesis is suspect. However, the kernel of an idea remains. It is important to intervene early and continuously to prevent significant numbers of each cohort from falling behind, which surely is an important, if not the sole, reason why so many leave school before graduating.

Process intervention points to the desirability of making use of Headstart, more flexibility in the first three grades to bring about a better fit between a child's learning readiness and the curriculum, and improved teaching and tutoring during the crucial next three years so that most inner-city youngsters are able to complete the first six grades at or close to national norms. This should be an important objective because it could set the stage for greater flexibility in pupil assignments to junior and senior high schools, which would have a more heterogeneous student body and would also be located outside of the most dilapidated neighborhoods.

Even if these recommendations were accomplished it would be desirable, in fact necessary, to follow them with another process intervention, this time among the fourteen- to eighteen-year olds—that is, during the high school years. A combination of curriculum weakness and teacher indifference would lead to serious questioning on the part of many young adolescents, even those at grade level, as to whether making the effort to be attentive in class, do their homework, and spend some time in outside reading are worthwhile. As noted earlier, many youngsters see no direct link between their future and what goes on in school and in their daily lives. Hence, it is important for various efforts—corporate, community, voluntary—to provide job exposure, work experience, and opportunities for earning some money to inner-city youngsters.

The aim of school/work programs should be to strengthen motivation: Students who perform in school and pass their courses should have priority in obtaining the part-time and/or summer jobs and being rewarded with other desirable opportunities. It does not follow, of course, that even if many of these links were forged and maintained over an extended period of time in order to provide a demonstration effect for the next cohort that the dropout rate would disappear. Clearly, it would not, but if an overwhelming number of young people entered the seventh grade without being behind grade, and this second process intervention were initiated at the eighth or ninth grade, the dropout rate should decline substantially, even precipitously. Most young people drop out of school because they are unable to learn, find school boring, and see no point in making an effort. These are the critical dimensions that process interventions must address.

As for macro-interventions, it is easy to identify a few that should be pursued even if they fall far short of a major sanitization of the pathological ghetto environment. The burgeoning efforts now under way to reduce the number of families whose head (mostly female) is more or less permanently on welfare is a move in the right direction. Children need early exposure to the relationship of work, income, and living standards.

It has been noted that the financing of public education should be restructured at least to the point where there are some extra funds available to school systems and principals to permit experimentation with curriculum improvement, the recruitment of young teachers for term appointments, etc. The major challenge before us is the need for a serious effort to expand work opportunities for in-school youth. The old entitlement project demonstrated that black youth in particular were able to improve their employment and earnings by a significant amount as a result of their participation. Unfortunately, this specific intervention failed to have more than a marginal influence on their high school completion rate, a not surprising conclusion given our emphasis on the need for process-type interventions. No matter how effective new and strengthened program, process, and macro-interventions turn out to be, there would inevitably be a considerable number of young people dropping out before earning their high school diplomas—hence, the need for strengthened second-chance opportunities.

The significant number of out-of-wedlock births to teenagers results in a sizable dropout rate among young mothers. Although some cities encourage these young women to continue in special schools during pregnancy and to return to school after they have given birth, this is not the norm. Pregnant teenagers and young mothers need more and better second-chance opportunities.

Another group in need of assistance are young drug addicts and/or offenders, many of whom leave school lacking the skills required for regular employment. One serious problem in most states is the severe shortage of useful educational and skill acquisition programs for offenders who are institutionalized. Unless their levels of knowledge and skills can be increased while they are in custody, it is likely that once they are released, they will return to their old haunts and activities.

A third group that requires access to second-chance opportunities are immature youngsters who drop out at seventeen or so without a diploma and who, as a result of age and experience, recognize at twenty or later the desirability of getting their GED.

Although most large cities currently have some second-chance opportunities available for one or more of these groups, recent discussions with UCLA professor, Arthur Cohen, the nation's leading authority on community colleges, called attention to the substantial neglect of community colleges to serve school dropouts and the hard-to-employ. He noted the opposition in several states to paying twice for education— via support for high schools and again via support for community colleges!

In sum, the high school dropout problem is severe, and the intervention efforts to date have been grossly inadequate because they have not seriously focused on process interventions. If the twelve-year developmental cycle (fifteen-years counting preschool) fails to perform effectively, it should not be surprising to find that most "repair" efforts prove to be only modestly effective. Effort should be focused on ensuring that the defective developmental cycle is strengthened and reinforced.

Youth Unemployment

There are several distinct but interrelated reasons why an advanced society should be deeply concerned about the continuing high levels of youth unemployment. First of all, Youth, especially those from low-income homes, need the opportunity to earn some income in their adolescent years to help them assume slowly the responsibilities and attitudes of adulthood. In the absence of such opportunities to work and earn income, many youth are likely to seek alternative sources of income from illicit and illegal activities including violent crime, which places persons other than themselves at risk of life, limb, or loss of property. In turn, a society must apprehend, commit, and incarcerate the more serious offenders and this results in a sizable societal cost. Many first offenders become recidivists in part because they lack the skills to obtain regular jobs.

A U.S. Nobel laureate in economics once argued that youth unemployment was not a serious societal problem because, as he said, it is well known that unemployment rates decline radically for men and women when they are in their twenties. I countered by pointing to the large number of young people who are in jail, the high homicide rate, the increasing number of black males who are not in the labor force, and the growing number of unemployed teenagers who make only a marginal adjustment to work in later life.

The following provides a brief overview of interventions directed to reducing youth unemployment, set within our analytic matrix.

1. There are sizable voluntary and governmental programs in most large cities aimed at providing summer jobs for disadvantaged youth although federal funding has been reduced since the Reagan administration took office.

2. A limited number of states and some cities have allocated funds for year-round youth employment programs, usually tied to public works (parks, clean-up operations and the like), but the totality of these efforts is quite small compared to the Public Service Employment (PSE) effort when the Comprehensive Employment and Training Act (CETA) was in effect.

3. There are a limited number of process interventions, mostly funded by foundations, that focus on encouraging young people to remain in school until graduation and that provide them with part-time and summer jobs (for example, the Edna McConnell Clark Foundation).

4. The large-scale "macro" efforts at job creation of the Youth Act of 1977 and CETA's PSE, which were phased out early in the first Reagan administration, have had no real success. What we have instead is a 40 percent set-aside in the JPTA training program, which is just that—training without stipends. More importantly, as noted earlier, JPTA is directed to preparing job-ready applicants, which means that in many cities the most seriously disadvantaged do not represent more than a small proportion of youth enrollees.

5. In terms of second-chance opportunities, the Job Corps, residential and nonresidential, remains an important but not a very large resource, providing about 40,000 slots annually. The recent efforts of many states to engage in welfare-conversion in an effort to find funding to encourage women to leave the welfare rolls via training and short-term subsidized

employment should be noted, but for the most part these work/welfare efforts are directed to a comparatively older group of women.

6. When Congress recently passed a small CCC program fashioned after the California Conservation Corps program, the president vetoed it on the ground that the federal government has no legitimate role in job creation. Job creation, he argued, is a task of the private sector.

7. The armed services have long provided opportunities for employment, training, and benefits to a significant proportion of minority youth, and they still do. But over the years, the military has paralleled the corporate sector in accepting overwhelmingly only high school graduates. Therefore, the armed services no longer represent opportunity for those disadvantaged youths most in need of a second chance.

Finally, the economy has remained quite slack even after four years of expansion, with unemployment around 7 percent, the underemployment rate closer to 14 percent, youth unemployment in the 20 percent range, and minority youth unemployment double that and even higher.

Concluding Observations

The excessive level of school dropouts among inner-city minority youth, their disturbingly high unemployment rate, and their subsequent marginal attachment to the regular work force are interrelated and should be seen as a single problem of severe social maladjustment. Our increasingly service-based economy (which provides three out of every four jobs) has progressively fewer openings for individuals who do not have a high school diploma or its equivalent. The problem is compounded by the continuing inflow of immigrants who are willing to compete for any unskilled openings that are available.[7]

In the late 1970s, a period of relatively liberal federal financing of training and job programs for youth, the issue of educational remediation (as a result of dropping out of school) was not well integrated with training and work opportunities, and little attention was directed to moving young people into regular jobs. Most of the federal effort then must be viewed as income-maintenance rather than employment focused.

But even if all of these shortcomings were remedied and if large federal funds again became available, the effort would not succeed in the face of a 20 to 40 percent unemployment level for youth. As no administration is likely to run the economy tight in the next few years, the only alternative is for the federal government, in association with the states, to launch and maintain significant job creation programs that would provide employment for young people (and adults as well) in the public sector as long as the private sector did not have jobs available for all who wanted and needed to work. Although such a program would not be inexpensive, it would be well within the resources of our society if we decided that large numbers of unemployed minority youth and adults represent an alternative that should not be tolerated.

Notes

1. Eli Ginzberg and Douglas W. Bray, *The Uneducated* (New York: Columbia University Press, 1953).

2. Eli Ginzberg, with the assistance of J. K. Anderson, D. W. Bray, and Robert W. Smuts, *The Negro Potential* (New York: Columbia University Press, 1956).

3. The Twentieth Century Task Force on Employment Problems of Black Youth (Eli Ginzberg, chairman), *The Job Crisis for Black Youth* (New York: Praeger Publishers, 1971).

4. National Commission for Employment Policy (Eli Ginzberg, chairman), *Tell Me About Your School* (Washington, D.C.: 1979).

5. Albert Rees, "An Essay on Youth Joblessness," *Journal of Economic Literature* 24(1986):613–628.

6. James S. Coleman et al., *Equality of Educational Opportunity* (Washington, D.C.: GPO, 1966); and James S. Coleman et al., *Youth: Transition to Adulthood* (Chicago: University of Chicago Press, 1974).

7. Thomas R. Bailey, *Immigrant and Native Workers: Contrasts and Competition* (Boulder, Colo.: Westview Press, 1987).

7

Directions for Policy

Probably the most important finding from the foregoing chapters is that a large number of individual, family, institutional, and societal forces singly and collectively operate to damage the developmental experiences of large numbers of children and young people. As a consequence of serious shortcomings in their immediate environment during the critical years of their growing up, many young people reach the threshold of adulthood poorly prepared to meet the performance requirements of a citizen in the United States in 1987.

Although the family and school head the list of critical structures that fail the young, identifying them obscures almost as much as it reveals. If one examines why so many families and schools do not educate their students to an appropriate level of competence, multiple explanations compete for attention and no one commands broad acceptance.

One commonly identified factor is the persistence of racism in U.S. society. The pervasiveness of racial discrimination in its multiple dimensions can be seen in the crippling of the psyches of many young children resulting in low self-esteem and a damaged ego, a great amount of repressed anger (which often breaks out once adult controls are no longer effective), and other emotional defects and disorders.

It takes little sophistication to tie the prevalence of racism to the poor economic circumstances of many minority black and Hispanic families, particularly those in which no father, real or adopted, is present in the household. The absence of a husband in many families where young children are growing up often reflects the difficulties that many minority men face in acquiring the attitudes and behavior that would enable them to obtain a steady job, to earn a reasonable wage, and to progress in their career. Lacking these attributes they sooner or later become marginal persons failing to make or maintain family ties. The absence of the male from the family and his inability to contribute to its upkeep are the most important reasons why so many minority youngsters are growing up in households mired in poverty.

The absence of a father points up the unhappy choice that many female heads of households face: to exist on welfare with its many shortcomings and indignities or to try to find and hold a job that would enable the family to get off welfare. Because many minority women have limited skills, the jobs available to them are at the low end of the wage scale and often fail to pay enough to enable the family to escape from the welfare rolls. Moreover, a mother of one or two children, especially young children, who seeks to hold down a full-time job, in the absence of special circumstances such as a nonworking adult in the household, would be seriously pressed for time and energy to do both— to rear her family and to work.

Racism, poverty, and single parentage are three powerful deterrents to the establishment of the protective and supportive environment that children need to help them develop and mature. But the reach of these disabilities extends beyond the immediacy of parent-child relationships, critical as these are.

Consider that race and family income are the powerful determiners of where people live and the quality of the housing available to them. Even before children enroll in the first grade they are influenced by the values and behavior of their neighbors and friends. We know that large numbers of minority poor, especially in dense urban concentrations, live in highly dysfunctional neighborhoods where drugs, crime, prostitution, vandalism, and assault are the order of the day and where mobsters, pimps, prostitutes, and drug dealers are often the only persons who have been able to raise themselves out of poverty and provide the only prototypes of successful individuals.

The combined inputs of race, poverty, single parenthood, adverse neighborhoods, and distorted values contribute a great deal to the malfunctioning of the local school. Educating the young requires the support and encouragement of interested and concerned parents who are in the best position to impress on their children the critical importance of adopting a positive attitude toward learning including the discipline required to do their homework, avoid truancy, and to learn to read for pleasure. Although a rare school may be able on its own to capture the imagination and participation of the young, it is generally recognized that parental support often makes the difference between the school's success and failure. And many minority families in low-income areas, fortunately by no means all, are unable to provide this critical support.

To continue this summary about how the development process fails so many minority youth: Many young people early come to view the school as a "shuffle," an institution aimed at keeping them in their place—at the periphery of society, eligible only for the least demanding and rewarding jobs. Small wonder that they make little or no effort to learn and early start to be truants, looking forward to the time when the law will set them free.

As they reach early adolescence they need opportunities to earn spending money, but such opportunities are hard to come by in the neighborhoods where they live unless they are willing to engage in illicit or illegal activities. Many decide that the risk is worth it, but over time many get caught and develop a police record that will still further reduce their prospects of obtaining regular jobs, now or in the future. Early sex has great attraction to both young men and young women, caught as they are in an environment that promises little reward for delayed gratification. Many young women who become pregnant decide against an abortion on the ground that having a child may add meaning and direction to their lives through motherhood and setting up an independent household, even if welfare pays the bills. The combined ravages of growing up without a father, in poverty, attending an unresponsive school, being exposed to the pathology of the ghetto, suffering the indignities of pervasive racism, and unable when they reach working age to find a regular job are reflected in the homicide rates of young black males. Homicide is the single largest cause of death among black men aged fifteen to twenty-four; its frequency is six times greater than that for white males and as much as a hundred times greater than the rate in selected Western European countries.

Before we explore the basic theme of this concluding chapter—whether and to what extent prevention is possible—we will recapitulate briefly the policy interventions that have sought to mitigate if not eliminate the major sources of weakness in the developmental experiences of minority youth in the post–World War II era.

Federal-state liberalization of the AFDC program made it possible for most single parents to keep and rear their offspring even if the level of dollar and in-kind aid has kept most of these families at or below the poverty level.

Federal, state, and local governmental programs via grants, loans, tax advantages, and other benefits led to the construction of considerable public housing. Some of these projects, through the selection of families in greatest need, introduced such a high level of concentrated pathology that sooner or later forces their abandonment.

Federal, state, and local governments have increased their per pupil school expenditures in low-income areas substantially since 1965, although not to a point where most of them are at levels comparable to schools in middle-class neighborhoods, despite the greater needs of the ghetto youngsters. The financial barriers to attend community and four-year public colleges were lowered and in many cases removed. Federal-state appropriations for Medicaid starting in 1966 substantially increased the access to health services of many poor minority adults, adolescents, and children—but primarily for short-term acute care.

In the years 1962 to 1981 the federal government spent approximately $100 billion on employment and training programs, primarily for adults, but these programs also included the Job Corps, the summer youth program, and the entitlement program, which were focused on minority youth.

In addition to these major governmental interventions aimed at ameliorating the life circumstances of the poor and expanding the opportunity structure for their offspring, we must also note the considerable efforts of the corporate and voluntary sectors, which made varying but often sizable contributions along several fronts. These efforts included improving local schools; providing family planning services; facilitating the employment of the hard-to-employ; providing financial assistance for neighborhood development projects; and supporting preventive, therapeutic, and rehabilitative services for various groups of adolescents and young adults at high risk such as ex-offenders, former drug addicts, and many others in need of special assistance.

The question that arises is how can we explain in the face of these considerable and sustained public and private efforts why teenage pregnancy resulting in births to unmarried mothers is increasing; why school dropouts among minority youth remain at the 50 percent level; why the use of alcohol and crack among young people is rising; why drunk driving is the principal cause of death among young people; and why homicide is the principal cause of death among minority youth and young adults. In order to explain these problems a trial balance sheet must take note of the following:

- The predominant number of sexually active young women among minority groups do not become teenage mothers. No more than about one in three does.
- Despite the sizably increased expenditures per pupil in daily average attendance, the capacity of most ghetto schools to teach basic skills remains grossly deficient. In the absence of effective learning, many youngsters become turned off, tuned out, and drop out as soon as the opportunity offers.
- The accident and death rates from driving have declined precipitously over the post–World War II period. However, the continuing high loss of life among adolescents and young adults reflects not only easy access to alcohol and cars but also the immaturity and skill deficiencies of youth and recently licensed drivers.

- The distortions of growing up without the presence of a father; the corrosive effects of racism; the ease with which young people are able to acquire guns; and the lawlessness of the environment in which they live go far to explain the lack of restraint of young blacks in the taking of human life.

This balance sheet may be suspect for its simplicity, but one cannot disregard these facts as we move to the question of the potential of prevention and the final challenge of pointing new directions for policy.

The thrust of our detailed analysis of drunk driving, teenage pregnancy, drug users, and dropouts suggests why "prevention" is likely to be a difficult form of intervention. As noted earlier, our society is highly dependent on access to the automobile for work and play, and alcohol is a drug of preferred use among the U.S. population second only to cigarettes. One can do a great many things to alert young people (and their parents) to the danger of driving after drinking; and one can even change some of the societal rules and patterns of behavior (raising the drinking age and the conditions for granting licenses) with an aim of reducing the number of drunk drivers. But short of a return to interdicting all alcoholic beverages and raising the age at which auto licenses are granted, educational efforts remain the principal tool available. We can learn to make better use of informational-educational approaches, but it is problematic that such efforts will contribute more than modest reductions in the short and middle term. There is no effective preventive device against immature risk-taking behavior and beginners' limitations of skill.

In the case of teenage pregnancy leading to unwed motherhood, the outlook for primary prevention is bleak, but we may be close to a breakthrough when it comes to secondary prevention. There is little prospect that the trend toward early sexual experience will be reversed. The best that one can anticipate is some months of delay, from an average in the case of young minority women of first intercourse at late fifteen to early or middle sixteen. There is surely opportunity for more effective instruction in the use of contraceptive devices, particularly the pill. But under the best of circumstances many young women will continue to become pregnant and a considerable proportion of them, especially among young minority women, will not seek an abortion.

French investigators have recently reported on a new drug RU486 that blocks the action of progesterone, a hormone essential to maintaining pregnancy. If a woman takes the drug orally within ten days of a missed menstrual period, abortion will be induced in about 85 percent of cases. With time, this percentage should increase and the side effects (not serious) should be brought under better control. The prospects for a significant decline in births to unwed teenagers have suddenly become much improved.

The current hysteria about adolescents who use drugs is not supported by our review of the evidence. In terms of long-term insidious effects, smoking and alcohol are probably the most dangerous habits that young people acquire in their early or late teens. Aside from the increasing use of crack, there is little solid evidence that many youngsters get hooked on dangerous drugs, or that many of them move from the use of marijuana, which is widespread, to hard drugs.

The threat each drug poses must not be minimized but neither should it be exaggerated. The much lower cost of crack compared to regular cocaine and the speed with which a user can become addicted should suffice to alert all communities that they face a new and serious problem, the answer to which will not come easily. The record is clear that the United States has failed to interdict the inflow and sale of addictive drugs, and there is little prospect that much larger and more costly efforts will succeed, given the high returns to violators as well as to many law enforcement officials.

Aside from the long-term antismoking campaign that has been under way for a quarter of a century and that commands widespread and increasing public support, there is little evidence that any of the variety of primary and secondary prevention programs aimed at keeping young people from addictive drugs has had, or is likely to have, great success. Fortunately most young people do not move from experimenting with hard drugs to becoming habitual users and addicts. A sizable number, however, become engaged in buying and selling drugs, an activity that often leads to criminal behavior resulting in injury, imprisonment, or death.

The last specific case that we analyzed involved school dropouts, the proportion of which among minorities remains in the 50 percent range. The primary prevention effort directed to moderating this serious personal and social failure has been preschool programs such as Headstart, supplemented by such secondary prevention approaches as greater flexibility in the curriculum during the first three years to accommodate children at different levels of readiness to learn, smaller classes, special coaching, make-up classes, alternate schools, and still other mechanisms that are directed to helping young people keep the pace. The 50 percent dropout rate in many inner-city schools is testimony to the modest success of the last quarter century of intensified efforts to bring the minority school dropout population closer to the white rate, which is about 15 percent nationally.

Can preventive interventions substantially reduce or preferably elim-inate the high losses to individuals and society that result from drunk driving, teenage pregnancy, the use of drugs, and teens dropping out of school? Cautious answers follow: Continuing public efforts involving parents, the police, legislation, and the media should be able to make inroads into the severe losses of life and limbs among teenage drivers and their victims. With respect to teenage pregnancy, primary prevention based on delaying sexual intercourse among young women holds limited promise. But expanded information about the informed use of contraceptives and the potentials of the new abortifacient drug may go far to reduce the upward trend in the numbers of unwed teenaged mothers.

There has been some success in a reduction of smoking among both young men and young women; some are still taking it up, but at a later age. The use of alcohol among young teens is probably greater than it has been, but the preferred drink among teenagers is beer, and most states have recently moved to raise the drinking age to twenty-one. Except for the recent scourge of low-cost cocaine (crack), most young people do not make regular use of addictive hard drugs. There is reason to believe that more adolescents and young adults may be at risk from dealing drugs than from using them, for trafficking in drugs is a prelude to a criminal career.

No primary nor secondary prevention interventions hold promise of cutting the frightening waste that results from 50 percent of all young people in an inner city failing to graduate from high school. Most of them have failed to acquire functional literacy without which they will be condemned to employment in only marginal jobs; and many of them will be unable to meet the other demands of citizenship in an increasingly complex technological society. The nation has experimented with a great number of programs aimed at improving public education and providing second-chance opportunities for those whom the schools have failed, but exceptional programs aside, these intervention efforts have fallen far short of what is needed.

It should now be clear why the "prevention paradigm" borrowed from the medical care arena is not the answer that many reformers and philanthropists expected it to be in reducing the level of ineffective performance among adolescents and young adults. The great success of the prevention approach in medicine dates from an earlier period when most disability and premature death resulted from virulent infections. Once children and adults could be vaccinated and immunized against the specific pathogen—smallpox, measles, infantile paralysis, and other devastating diseases—or once powerful antibiotics could be employed to curb the progress of debilitating and often fatal infections such as rheumatic fever, influenza, or pneumonia—and many others, the gains from primary and secondary prevention were there for all to see. The cost-benefit rates were so favorable that the societal response was overwhelmingly positive.

But the great success of primary prevention is now a matter of past achievement rather than current reliance even in the medical arena. Today most people who are afflicted, as well as many who die prematurely, do so as the consequence of one or more chronic conditions, particularly the malfunctioning of the heart, the kidneys, or the immune system. And there are no prevention techniques, only the reduction of risk factors, that speak directly to these major chronic diseases. Heavy smoking, the abuse of alcohol, excessive weight, and lack of exercise over long periods of time contribute to the possibility but do not ensure that people pursuing a dysfunctional life-style will be stricken.

As noted throughout this book, the ineffective performance of adolescents and young adults is a consequence of dysfunctional components of the developmental cycle starting from conception and birth to their eighteenth or twenty-first year. The absence of a father in the household; living in poverty, often on welfare; growing up in a disorganized ghetto area; suffering the indignities of racism; attending malfunctioning schools; bereft of models of successful relatives, friends, and neighbors; exposed from early age to violence and crime; unable to meet most employer's hiring requirements—and the many additional societal pathogens that militate against normal growth and development in the ghetto—all coalesce to produce ineffective performance. The amazing fact is not that so many young people growing up in such adverse conditions fall off the track by becoming pregnant in early adolescence, resorting to drugs, becoming school dropouts, or opting for a life of crime, but that such a large number manage, despite their cumulative hardships, to find a place for themselves in a society that has failed to provide them with anything like the range of opportunities available to young people growing up in middle-class families.

This observation about the much larger number of young people who are at risk relative to the numbers who fail helps to explain why the preventive approach is so severely limited. There is no way that even a benevolent society, which wanted to reduce human wastage by adopting strong intervention devices early in the life of a child growing up under severely disadvantaged circumstances, would be able to identify those most likely to fail so that it could start on a corrective program. And no society, even one as affluent as the United States, has shown the desire, much less the will, to tax away such a large part of the earnings of the rich and the middle class in order to correct inequality of opportunity for minority youth.

Whether the effort, if made, would succeed is problematic, but it is surely not on the nation's agenda at present, nor is it likely to be added in the near and middle term.

If prevention is not the answer and a radical redistribution of income aimed at creating even a rough equality of opportunity for minority youth is not in the cards, what can and should be done by a society that has a measure of good will and commitment to reduce ineffective performance among minority youth?

Racism continues to extract a heavy toll. Accordingly, it is imcumbent on all sectors of U.S. society, and especially on its leaders, to work toward its eradication by any and all means available to them in both the public and the private spheres of life. Large gains have been made since World War II to eliminate segregation and to reduce discrimination, but a great deal still remains to be done. Martin Luther King near the end of his life looked forward to the elimination of all forms of discrimination in the labor market by the year 2005. In the absence of a revised public commitment and action we will not meet his goal.

There is no possibility for the normalization of minority family life unless both men and women are afforded an opportunity to work and support themselves and their dependents. At no time since the end of World War II, not even at the height of our involvement in Vietnam (1969) has the economy provided jobs for all who needed and wanted to work. Many members of minority groups because of their inferior education and erratic work experience exacerbated by widespread discrimination against them have found themselves at the end of the hiring queue. For the last seven years the U.S. economy has run slack and is likely to continue to run slack with the result that large numbers of younger and older members of minority groups will be unable to get and keep a regular job.

Many economists believe that we have not learned to run the economy taut and at the same time avoid inflationary pressures. Even if one accepts this pessimistic formulation, it does not preclude the federal government's instituting a publicly financed job program at minimum wages that would be open to all who need and want to work. The public is right to be disquieted by the large numbers who are on welfare or on other income transfer programs; and the still larger numbers who are engaged in illicit and illegal activities. But they can't have it both ways. They can protect and strengthen the work ethic but only if there are jobs, private or public, for all who want and need to work. Support for the work ethic in the face of a continuing shortfall of jobs is a mockery of the poor, the overwhelming proportion of whom seek the opportunity to work.

The third major challenge confronting public policy is the improvement of inner-city schools so that minority youth will obtain at least the minimum preparation required for them to make the transition into the world of work, adulthood, and citizenship. It would be not only foolish but wrong to minimize the difficulties of effecting the changes required, the recommendations of the many committees and commissions on strengthening the schools notwithstanding. But the speedier the progress the nation makes in pushing back the ugly inheritance of racism, and the quicker it moves to provide employment opportunities for all, the better the prospects for significant reforms in the educational performance of inner-city youth. The reduction of racism would contribute greatly to normalizing the goals and values of minority youth to a point where they would recognize the importance of taking school seriously as a prelude to a job, a career, and a better life. And if most minority adults were able to get and hold jobs and earn incomes, the disorganization of many families reflecting the absence of the male parent and dependency on welfare would be much reduced. Young people growing up in self-supporting two-parent families are much more likely to have a positive view of themselves, their schooling, and their future. Many additional reforms in the public educational system would be needed but the prospects of securing them would be greater if families and the community were normalized.

Once children and young people have been seriously damaged as a result of inadequate nurturing and lack of access to developmental opportunities, there are only a limited number of societal interventions that can hope to contain and reverse the outcomes of twenty years of cumulative deprivation. The answer to the question "Is prevention possible" is both no and yes. No—if we mean low-cost or even high-cost interventions such as more liberal income transfers and more Headstart programs. Yes—if society addresses the root causes of ineffective performance, racism, unemployment, and malfunctioning schools, all of which reinforce the inability of many minority families to nurture their young so that they are able to become self-supporting adults capable in turn of discharging their responsibilities as parents, workers, and citizens.

About the Authors

Eli Ginzberg is director, Conservation of Human Resources, and A. Barton Hepburn Professor Emeritus of Economics, Columbia University. He is the author or editor of numerous books on manpower economics, including *Medicine and Society* (Westview, 1987) and *The Skeptical Economist* (Westview, 1987). He is also coauthor of *Technology and Employment* (Westview, 1986).

Howard S. Berliner, Sc.D., is associate research scholar at Conservation of Human Resources, Columbia University. He is the author of *Strategic Factors in U.S. Health Care* (Westview, 1987) and *A System of Scientific Medicine: Philanthropic Foundations in the Flexner Era* (1985).

Miriam Ostow is senior research scholar, Conservation of Human Resources, Columbia University. She is coauthor of *Local Health Policy in Action* (1985) and *Home Health Care* (1984).

Index